THE
RAISING SHANE
WORKBOOK

KATE ROSEMARY

PUBLISHED BY WESTVIEW, INC., NASHVILLE, TENNESSEE

© 2005, 2008 Kate Rosemary. All Rights Reserved.
No portion of this book may be reproduced in any fashion,
either mechanically or electronically,
without the express written permission of the author.
Short excerpts may be used with the permission of the author
or the publisher for the purposes of media reviews.
Contact kate.rosemary@recycleddreams.org

ISBN 1-933912-49-9

First Edition, April 2008.
Front Cover Photograph by Kate Rosemary.
Back Cover Photograph by Ben Spiegel, Used by Permission of Kathleen Nelson Spiegel.
Photographs pages 83, 122 and 162 by Michael Horton Photography (www.michaelhortonphotography.com). Used by Permission.
Other Known Photograph Credits on pages 166 and 167
Typography by Mary Catharine Nelson.
Printed in the United States of America on acid free paper.

PUBLISHED BY WESTVIEW, INC.
P.O. Box 210183
Nashville, Tennessee 37221
www.publishedbywestview.com

THANK YOU

TO SHANE
WHO PREFERS TO BE KNOWN AS "THE WONDERFUL MAGNIFICENT"
You changed my life for the better.

TO SHANE'S FAVORITE ADVERSARY AND BEST ALLY, JAY
Who Gave Our Family the Gift of Words

TO SHANE'S MOST DETERMINED TUTOR, SHERRY
Whose Generosity and Patience Helped Make a Happy Ending Possible

TO MY MOTHER, SHANE'S GRANNY, ALLISON
For the Title That Got Me Started

TO SHANE'S EVER-ACCOMMODATING COLLABORATOR, DAVID
Provider of Shane's Paycheck and Best Motivation to Get Out of Bed

TO SHANE'S ADVOCATES: KELLYE, CINDY, STEPHANIE, MARY, AND KATHY
Social Workers and Match Makers Who Paired a Headstrong Woman with an Almost Equally Recalcitrant Boy

TO THE REST OF SHANE'S DOCTORS, TEACHERS, TUTORS, AND FRIENDS
Without Whom We Would Never Have Survived

TO ALL OF SHANE'S BROTHERS AND SISTERS, ESPECIALLY
NOEL, MARY, ALEX, JOHN, BRIDGETT, ROZITA, RYAN, JASON, AND JESSIE
Who Have Stories of Their Own

TO ALL THE PARENTS WHO RAISE CHILDREN JUST LIKE HIM
Because I Cannot Possibly Adopt Them All

AND

TO STONEWALL
For Everything

DEDICATION

Shane has been an inspiration to many who have known him. Though it may take him a little longer to do things than most people, he is a living testimony to our ability to do anything we set our minds to and work towards with all our hearts.

For the two years that he studied for the TCAP (the exam required for a regular high school diploma in our state), Shane dedicated himself to doing nothing else. He would get up in the morning, wash the family's dishes, study at home alone all day while I went to work, and then go to his tutor's at night. For two years, he took the test every single time it was given. He simply refused to give up.

Time after time, he has risen above the limitations others tried to place upon him. He has taken on overwhelming odds – and won.

It has been an honor and a privilege to be his mother.

SHANE MURRAY, THIS BOOK IS FOR YOU.

With All My Love, From Your Mom, On This, the 16th Day of May 2005.

INTRODUCTION

About This Book

If you are thinking about fostering or adoption, this is a good book to start with. It doesn't offer beautiful pictures of waiting infants or angelic toddlers. Those, you can get from any agency. Instead, in fifty-two short chapters on different topics related to adoption and foster care, this book invites you to consider and prepare for realistic possibilities your agency may not think to mention.

This book is written from the point of view of a foster and adoptive parent who has found the experience to be fulfilling, rewarding, gratifying, and exhausting! In the thirty years between 1977 and 2007, the author parented one birth son, two stepsons, three foster daughters, one foster son, and three adopted sons. Most of these young people presented with some combination of characteristics that put them in a category known as "special needs" or "hard to place."

These characteristics included being older than five at the time of placement (the youngest was six and the oldest eighteen), being in a racial minority (one daughter and one son), and being part of a sibling group (the two youngest brothers). Their medical and psychiatric diagnoses include Posttraumatic Stress Disorder, Reactive Attachment Disorder, Major Depression, Physical Abuse, Manic Depression with Psychotic Episodes, Hemophilia that resulted in AIDS from a blood transfusion, Multiple Personality Disorder (now known as Disassociative Identity Disorder), Obsessive-Compulsive Disorder, Intermittent Explosive Disorder, Addiction, Sexual Abuse, Attention Deficit Hyperactivity Disorder, Borderline Intellectual Functioning, Sociopathy, Hypertension, Failure to Thrive, Hearing Impairment, Rickets, and Polycystic Kidney Disease.

••

Each topic is illustrated by an example from the life of one of the author's adopted sons. The chapters are arranged so that the illustrations are in chronological order according to when the events occurred. All of the episodes in the narrative are about some aspect of raising Shane.

Shane was placed into the care of the state when he was five years old. Between that day and his placement with the author on the day before his tenth birthday, he was moved twenty-one times.

Some of the stories are funny. Some are tragic. All are true.

••

The final section of each chapter contains questions and ideas for your consideration. Consider this: You could read no more than one chapter each week and still finish the entire book within a year. You could *not* read the book, a year could go by anyway, and you might still be no better prepared for fostering or adopting than you are today. Or this: If you completed just one topic each five days, you'd be done in less time than it takes a physical pregnancy to reach full term. Shall we begin?

TABLE OF CONTENTS

Dedication v
Introduction - About This Book vii

1. Genesis - In the Beginning… 1
2. Preparations - Not Exactly an After-Thanksgiving-Dinner Nap 5
3. Commitments - I Did WHAT? 8
4. Neediness - Deprivation 12
5. Complications - Familial Ecology 15
6. Physicians - The Vampire Lady in Andersonland 18
7. Therapists - Pre-Shrink, Shrink, Shrank, Shrunk 20
8. Legalities - Contracts and Expectations 24
9. Self Care - Heal Me, Please 27
10. Anger - What's That You Say? 30
11. Rejection - "I'm Biting Your Motherrrr!" 33
12. Compassion - Moses 36
13. Play - Possum Stew 39
14. Discernment - Twiko 42
15. Forgiveness - This Time It Wasn't the Cat that Ate the Canary! 45
16. Revelations - Holocaust 48
17. Fidelity - You Can Run, but You Cannot Hide 51
18. Grief - Angela 54
19. Motivation - Eat Your Words 57
20. Guardian Angels - Sisyphus 60
21. Flexibility - Along Came a Spider… 64
22. Gratification - Breakthrough 67
23. Stability - You Just Don't Get Another Mother 70
24. School Phobia - Broken Arms 73
25. Vacations - Buddha, the Boy 76
26. Naming - And the Winner Is… 80
27. Goals - Finger Lickin' Chicken 83
28. Change - Chef 85
29. Laughter - Horse Sense 88
30. Medical Care - The Bad Patient 90
31. Surrender - Shane and Earline Throw a Party 93
32. Reciprocity - Adult Day Care 98
33. Love - 43 Minutes, More or Less 101
34. Happenstances - Failed Mediation 104
35. Catastrophe - Why Not Me? 107
36. Safety - Only Our Own Idiot Doctor Will Do 111

37.	Medication - Gratitude	114
38.	Creativity - Alternative Celebrations	117
39.	Independence - I Just Don't Trust People!	120
40.	Patience - How Did He DO That?	122
41.	Emancipation - You Never Know	125
42.	Reunions - Pomp and Circumstances	128
43.	Disruption - When Termination Comes before You're Ready	131
44.	Vulnerability - Used and Abused	134
45.	Support Systems - The Most Magnificent Tutor	137
46.	Focus - Practice Makes Perfect	140
47.	Activities - Buddha, the Dog	143
48.	Serendipity - He Gets By with a Little Help from His Friends	146
49.	Perseverance - Just When I Needed It Most	149
50.	Timing - The Nose Knows	152
51.	Setbacks - The Bridge	155
52.	Success - And a Good Time Was Had by All	158

Conclusion - A Final Note on Foster Care, Adoption, and Court ... 162
Postscript ... 165
Photographs ... 166

1. GENESIS

In the Beginning…

Each of us comes in a different way to the decision to parent children who are not our biological offspring. For most, the decision comes after multiple efforts at conception. For some, there were drug treatments for infertility, or attempts at artificial insemination. For many, there have been years of disappointment, in some circumstances including heartbreaking miscarriage or the tragic loss of children who survived birth only to die too soon. Others come at the decision from a different direction. Having had children of their own, or having decided not to for one reason or another, they choose to foster or adopt for moral, ethical, or other personal reasons. Sometimes those reasons are altruistic. Sometimes they are not.

Whatever brings you to contemplate this decision, there are many things to consider. If you already have children at home, the first thing you will want to think about is the effect an additional family member will have on those children. If you are making this decision as a couple, there is the question of how this addition would impact your relationship. If you are single, do you have the support you need to pull this off successfully?

While fostering or adopting an infant may, in many ways, duplicate the dynamics of the addition of a birth child, the addition of an older child will be drastically different. Many of the questions that will arise are the same as those that would come up if the child were born into your family – finances, family and community support, schools, doctors. Some questions apply to fostering and adopting equally, such as relationships with birth families or how to respond to wounding done to the child before s/he came into your home. Other questions are limited to adoptions – whom to tell that the child is adopted, when to tell, and what to tell.

*This book tells the story of one such family, walking potential parents through the stages, trials, struggles and delights of parenting a special-needs child. Most of the issues that came up with this child will arise in some form (although likely to a lesser degree) with every fostered or adopted child, whether the child is considered to be special-needs, hard-to-place, or not. As you read, keep in mind that due to the severity of the trauma Shane experienced before he was adopted, many of these issues will **not** be as big of a problem for you and yours. Each part of Shane's story is true.*

••

Raising Shane was Noel's idea to begin with. Oh, he may not have had Shane in mind exactly, but it was his idea. When his father and I divorced and he was missing his two older stepbrothers (who stayed with their dad), he started lobbying with me for a little brother of his own. Or a sister. At that point, he didn't care who it was, or what race or sex it was, or even how old it was. All that really mattered then was that it play soccer. Noel loved soccer, and he thought that someone to play soccer with was just what he needed to make his life complete.

As Noel's mother, I was struggling to make it through graduate school at the time, and I made the kind of promise parents often make. It was a promise I expected never to have to make good on, because I believed he'd change his mind before the note came due.

Noel was only nine-turning-ten that summer, and the deal I made with him was this: just give me until I have graduated from school and have been working full time for two years to get my feet on the ground. Then I'll adopt you a brother or sister, as long as s/he is at least school age, so I don't have to do diapers or daycare again as a single parent. I promise. To be honest, I thought he'd quickly forget all about it, and soon, I actually did.

But Noel did not forget. Sure enough, four summers later, he announced to me that my time was almost up. What was I going to do about it, he wanted to know, and when? Pretending that I had *not*, in fact, forgotten, I got busy exploring the possibilities.

Although I had not spent a lot of time thinking about adoption, I was sure by that point in my life that I was not willing to adopt the kind of child who would be easy to find a home for. I knew that there were people lined up to adopt cute babies and adorable toddlers. My tenure at Vanderbilt Divinity School had solidified my belief that I was called to be a good steward of my emotional as well as my financial resources. The time I had spent working for CASA, the Court Appointed Special Advocate program for our local juvenile court, had exposed me to children who were horribly abused, difficult to find placements for, and who were often in need of adoptive homes. The years I had spent at the church I was attending then had exposed me to friends who set the example of adopting children who needed extraordinary placements. That was the type of child I believed I was called to parent.

There seemed no point in taking a child who would be easy to find a home for, because that kind of child would not need someone as stubborn as me. If I was willing to make a commitment to a child no matter what, it seemed that the most useful thing I could do was commit to a child who was not likely to find someone who would keep them, no matter what. The die was cast.

I started out by approaching the local office of the state Department of Children's Services, as I was interested in a program they had which provided subsidies and medical care for children in a category known as "hard to place." At the time, this included minority children over the age of two, Caucasian children over the age of five, sibling groups, and children with any type of handicapping condition. A class was required before one could qualify to adopt, and I started out by asking questions about what that entailed. It turned out that if one went through the state, then Noel, who was by that time a freshman in high school, would not be allowed to attend. The state's classes were for prospective parents only.

That was not okay with Noel, at least, who said he felt that if we were going to add another family member with problems, then he needed to be as well prepared as possible. Shopping around a bit more, I discovered that there was another local agency which not only allowed but also encouraged family members and other supportive friends to attend their adoption preparation classes with the potential adoptive parents. I decided, on that basis, to go with them. I signed up for the very next set of classes.

Sometime within the first couple of class meetings, each family in the group was given a sheaf of papers that had to be completed. The task seemed a daunting one. They wanted everything from a complete autobiography to a detailed list of what kind of child was acceptable. Unlike many of the potential parents in the class, my requirements were simple: the child had to be school age (I was not doing daycare again) and had to have the potential to leave home some day.

I was not asking for a guarantee, just for no problem that would mean that as a single parent, I would have to anticipate the necessity of caring for this family addition without help for the rest of my life. Just the potential to leave home was all I was asking for. Well, that, and no diapers.

It wasn't much to ask.

••

Consider…

What was it like growing up in your family of origin?

What leads you to contemplate fostering or adoption at this time in your life?

What are you hoping to offer a child?

What are you hoping a child or children will add to your family?

What characteristics are you willing to take on as a challenge?

Which ones are you not willing to accept?

What age range, sex, race and combination of special needs would be accepted by your family and community, and what is likely to be the response if you take on a child outside of those parameters?

NOTES

2. PREPARATIONS

Not Exactly an After-Thanksgiving-Dinner Nap...

It may be that you discover in the early stages of the process that there is additional work you must do to prepare for the arrival of an additional family member. For some prospective parents, this will mean that they discover they need to do additional work in therapy to work through issues of their own. These may include issues that have arisen in this process thus far, baggage carried on from childhood that may impair the ability to parent, or conflict between members of the couple that impact on their ability to parent together. For other potential parents, the work that must be done will require removing other impediments. Financial difficulties which would make it unwise to take on additional commitments at this time and changes to prepare one's home environment for additional members are two of those. There are undoubtedly others. Facing any changes in our lives can be sometimes fearful and at other times exciting. Once any obstacles are out of the way, miracles can happen.

• •

The holidays had arrived. My good friend Ingrid brought her son Isaac to join Noel and me for Thanksgiving. Ingrid was frequently a source of unconventional ideas, and while we were eating dinner, we talked about the anticipation of the coming child. At the time, my house had only two bedrooms, and I had been contemplating possibilities that might allow me to convert some of the space into a third.

While we were eating, Ingrid had an excellent idea: I could move the kitchen into the Florida room which was currently serving as Noel's bedroom, convert the old kitchen into his new bedroom, wall off one end of the dining/living room to make an additional bedroom for the coming child, and then open a door between what would be left of the living room and the den so that I could put the dining room in what had been serving as the den. If it sounds complicated, that is because it was. It was also an excellent idea. All the way through dinner I kept thinking about what the arrangement of the house would be if we did that. The more I thought about it, the more I liked it.

Finally, when dinner was over, we began talking about what we wanted to do for the rest of the day. The boys wanted to play video games, and Ingrid wanted to take a walk. When it came to me, I said that what I'd really like to do was to tear out the wall between the living room and the den to see what it would be like for the room to open in that direction. Ingrid laughed first, but said she was game to try it; the boys decided they would just stay out of our way.

I've always loved construction work, ever since I did my first project while I was in college, and I couldn't wait to get my hammer out again. We found a hammer for Ingrid, too, and she and I proceeded to get inside the closet on the den side of the wall that I intended to remove. I thought that would be a great place to start, so that if I found out there was brick or concrete under the drywall, it wouldn't look too bad until I could fix it. Since several of the interior walls in my older house were brick, I wouldn't be able to tell what this one was until I got into it.

Ingrid and I started by making a hole about four feet up from the floor, right in the center of the back wall of the closet, and worked our way outwards from there. In the center, it was drywall over studs. We found an opening wide enough for a door and kept going – by that time I was thinking I might just take out the entire wall – but just to either side of the four-foot opening, we discovered concrete. About that time I started to be worried that perhaps I had just found an old window, and that I wouldn't be able to make a doorway after all.

We started tearing out the drywall going downward, and discovered that the opening went all the way to the floor. Once we had cleared away all the refuse in that direction I stepped into the opening, with the drywall on the living room side still in place. The wall was about a foot thick, and you could see that there was brick on the living room side under the drywall. We tore out the framing that had been put into place to support the drywall, and I looked up. Above my head, sandwiched between the two walls, was a brick archway. I was standing in a doorway that had been hidden, just waiting to be revealed. I took it as a sign that it was meant to be.

••

Consider...

What obstacles keep you from being ready to parent at this time?

Are finances an issue? Check into the subsidies available to parents who adopt special-needs and hard-to-place children.

Do you need additional physical space or handicap accommodations? Ask whether or not the subsidy will cover these start-up expenses.

Do you have emotional issues that need to be addressed? Counselors are listed in the yellow pages.

What are you willing to do to address these impediments?

What would help you?

How can you access whatever it is you need?

When *can* you start?

When *will* you?

∾ NOTES ∾

3. COMMITMENTS

I Did WHAT?

Once the decision to foster or adopt is made, there are many preliminary steps before your child comes home. One of these is the home study, an invasive procedure in which every aspect of your home life is examined by an outsider. Each agency will have its own process, but typically the process will include multiple questionnaires, interviews and classes. If your decision is to accept an older child rather than an infant, you will likely be required to take a class to prepare you for issues (the new term for "problems") that will probably arise. Visits will be made to your home to ensure that you are able to provide a safe physical space for the child. If your goal is adoption, financial records will be required to see if you are financially able to take on the additional obligation.

*Typically, it is only after all these steps have been satisfactorily completed that you are presented with profiles of children the placement agency believes will be suitable for your home. The agency may or may not be forthcoming about the child's history and issues (read "problems"), and even if you **are** told everything the record shows, **no one** can predict what additional issues ("problems") will arise as the child ages. If this is an adoptive placement, you will want to request every written record available – the mother's health records from pregnancy, social services records and case notes, and school records. You want to know not just if the child was drug-affected at birth, but if the mother was using drugs at any time during the pregnancy. You need to talk to past and current foster parents, and any family members available. You need to find out everything you can in order to make an informed decision about whether or not to invite this child into your home.*

In the case of infant adoption, the birth mother frequently has the option of choosing the adoptive family. This means you may or may not be chosen for a child no matter what you have done up until this point, and no matter how wonderful a family you believe you could provide. In the case of foster and older children, it will be the child's worker and the agency staff who will decide the most suitable placement for each child. In that case, the child/ren may still have veto power over the placement once it is proposed. The waiting can be agony. It may also come to an end before you are ready.

Upon successful completion of the adoption preparation class and the home study, potential adoptive parents are presented with biographies, pictures, and stories of children who may be potential matches. In my case, I was presented with two children, siblings: Shane was a 9-year-old Caucasian male; his sister was 7 years old and biracial. Shane was diagnosed with Posttraumatic Stress Disorder (PTSD), Borderline Intellectual Functioning, and most descriptively, Intermittent Explosive Disorder. His sister, Tasha, was not.

These children were two out of a family of seven children, all of whom had been removed from the home because of tragic abuse at the hands of other family members. Shane was one of the two oldest, and consequently one of the two most wounded.

Shane had been "in the care of the state" for five years and had been moved twenty-one times. Tasha had been moved less frequently. For the previous year, she had been stable in the same foster home, while Shane had been in a group home run by the United Methodist Church in upper East Tennessee. By the time I came along, the other five children had already been divided up and placed for adoption in three other homes.

The special-needs adoption process allows potential parents the possibility of interviewing social workers, foster parents, and others who have had contact with the children while they have been in the care of the Department of Children's Services, and I talked to everyone I could find. I wanted to make sure I knew as much as possible about what I was getting myself into before I made a commitment. I talked at length to one of the other families that had adopted two of the siblings who were twins, and read case notes and medical records. I found out as much about the two children as I possibly could. It is important for adoptive parents to be sure about their commitment before meeting the children, because it is neither fair nor kind to any waiting child to meet them as though the potential parent is going shopping. I was determined to be certain. Finally, when I was absolutely sure, I let the children's social worker know that I was willing to commit, so that she could then start working with the children to see if they would have me as their mother.

The next time I went into the agency's office, the secretary joyfully greeted me, "Oh, so you're the one who is adopting the _____!" And she used a last name that I knew, oh-so-well, from my days at CASA.

"The _____?" I gasped. "I've agreed to adopt the _____?" I almost fell over with astonishment. I was so glad I heard the children's last name from her, first, rather than from one of them, because I was in that moment reeling from the thought… I did WHAT?

In the moment that I became aware of who they were, I realized that I knew more about these two children and their history than I could possibly have learned from their case notes and interviews. Completely without knowing it, I had agreed to adopt two children whose photographs had hung over my desk while I worked at CASA. I had kept their case files, and had known about the family's court battles. I had met their mother and their abusers, but all these years later, in one of those total mind blanks that sometimes happen, had never put the two families together. I had agreed to adopt two children that I had passing thoughts of adopting years before, when I had decided that I was in no way ready to do so. Time had brought them back into my life again.

Much to my disappointment, because by then I had emotionally committed to both of them, Tasha decided when approached that she wanted to remain with her foster mother to be adopted by her. She had been in that home for a year and did not want to be moved one more time, even if it meant that she could be placed again with her brother. Shane was devastated by her decision. He had lived through their separation on the promise that they would be placed for adoption together, and had already suffered so many losses that this one more was almost unbearable. However, as he has done so often in his life, he chose what was right for the one he loved rather than what was best for him. And so the decision was made, after years of trying to find the children a placement together, to separate them at the end once that placement had finally been found. Tasha would stay to be adopted by her foster mom, and Shane would come to me.

Consider...

Just as with efforts at conception, sometimes the foster/adoption process proves barren. Who in your life can support you as you wait?

If you have been presented with the profile of a child or children, who in their past can you contact? What questions are important for you to have answered before you make a commitment?

It is important that you make a commitment to the child/ren before you meet them, if possible. You cannot send birth children back after they arrive, and the threat of rejection is a burden that waiting children do not need to bear. After interviewing everyone available, are you ready to make the same commitment to this child or sibling group that you would to your own birth child, to love them until it is in the child/ren's best interest to go?

If your plan is to adopt an older child, you need to be prepared for the possibility that the child/ren may not want to join your family after they meet you, even after all you have done up till this point. How can you prepare yourself to be gracious and respect a child's decision for autonomy? Can you support him or her in the decision to wait for the right family to come along?

Once the match has been made, many foster and adoptive parents feel the same panic felt by birth mothers immediately before and after delivery – "I did WHAT? I'm not ready! Can I take it back?" If it helps any, the child is probably feeling many of the same feelings as you. What can help you ride the panic out and wait for it to subside?

❧ NOTES ☙

4. Neediness

Deprivation

No matter how hard you may try, it will be impossible to prepare yourself in advance for every need your child/ren will have. Many needs can be anticipated after meeting with the child's current caregivers, but others will not arise for years to come. One need you can plan on, though, is the need for your child to cling desperately to whatever possessions s/he beings to your home. Plan on respecting those possessions long after you think they should hit the trash. What looks to you like outgrown clothes or junk may be the only connection your child has to his or her past. That "trash" may be your child's history.

You can help your child make the transition to your home by preparing a place that has in it things your child loves. Photographs of family members, both biological family members and foster family members, can be enlarged and placed on the walls, reassuring a child that it is not necessary to give up those who are already loved in order to be a member of your family. These days, with a multitude of beds and furniture options, it is possible to design a room around a child's favorite things. A car bed, for instance, for a child who loves cars, can provide a feeling of welcome. Videotape of the adoptive home, family, extended family, and community can prepare the child to make the transition. Providing a space where a child can store his or her belongings until the time that s/he is ready to part with them can provide desperately needed continuity and safety for a child who has lost almost everything imaginable, including innocence.

It was hard to believe that in the United States anyone could have suffered the deprivation Shane evidenced. He was so afraid that there would not be food for the next meal that he would hide food in his room, just in case. He would refuse to eat one meal until we had gone over the menus for several meals to come and he had been shown and reassured that the food was actually available.

His meager belongings were so precious to him that he could not let go of them, just in case he didn't get more. Clothes that had long since been too small for him to wear were saved and treasured for years after they had last fit. He could save his money longer than any other child I have ever known, never spending it, just in case he needed it later.

Shane had even been deprived of normal childhood experiences. He would sit in my lap and explore my nose or ears like a toddler. He had lived in state custody for so long that he literally could not make choices. He could spend an hour or more trying to decide what to order from a menu. Shopping for clothes took more time than I could stand. Shopping for shoes was still worse, and he always chose them several sizes too large – just in case.

He had no sense of humor, not just in that he could not *make* a joke, but he could not *understand* one. Everything he heard was taken absolutely literally. We would try in vain to explain plays on words, but he just could not comprehend them.

Finally, Shane learned a joke, a trick, if you will. You have probably played it yourself, or had it played on you. Someone puts their finger on your shirt somewhere and asks, "What's that on your shirt?" When you look down, the person says, "Oops! Made you look!" and then slides a finger up to tap you on the bottom of your chin, or maybe your nose.

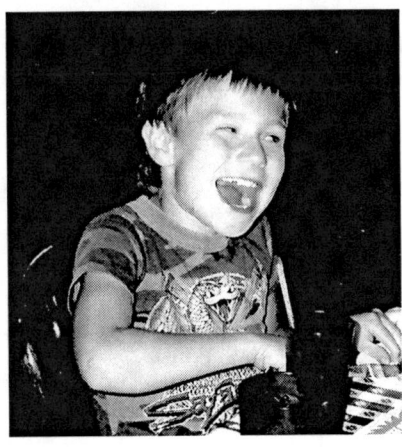

Once Shane learned this trick, he would play it for hours, over and over, and over again. Twenty, thirty times in a row or more, he would do it. The more he liked you, the more you got to experience it. And every time he did it, he would laugh as though it was the first time it had ever been played on anyone, anywhere, at any time.

Fifteen years later, he is doing it still.

Oh, excuse me. What's that on your shirt?

Oops! Made you look!

Consider...

Once you start to learn about the child/ren who will come to you, what can you do to make them feel welcome? What provisions can you make to respect your child/ren's ownership of the things they bring with them into your home?

What issues are likely to arise for your child/ren from the deprivation they experienced prior to coming to you?

Many times the extreme deprivation our child/ren experienced can trigger memories of our own losses and fears. In what sense does a child's loss or need bring up your own feelings of inadequacy, desperation, or despair?

❧ NOTES ☙

5. COMPLICATIONS

Familial Ecology

Most families have nine months to get ready for a new arrival. With rare exceptions, by that time the entire family is aware of the pregnancy and no further explanations are necessary. Adoptions and foster care don't exactly work that way. Sometimes the wait is long, and then the child/ren arrive quickly and unexpectedly. Other times, especially in foster care, the wait is so short that there is hardly time to make the bed before the child arrives.

If there are other children in the home, decisions have to be made regarding what they will be told about the newcomer. In cases of adoption, the receiving family has to make choices regarding their relationship with the birth family. Of these, what is in the child's best interest regarding continued contact with birth (and/or foster) family members is the most important. For foster children, that decision will be made by the placement agency. In adoption, depending on the age of the adopted child, other questions arise: What is an older child to be told about the new family? A video tape of the new home, church, mosque or synagogue, school, family and pets may help ease anxiety. If the child is an infant, what is the community to be told about the arrival? There was a time adopted infants were routinely passed off as birth children. Will that be the case here? Why or why not?

*Committing to parenting one child may **sound** like you're only adding one person to your family constellation, but when the child who is coming is older than an infant, the addition is likely to be much more complicated than you can possibly imagine. Whether continued contact is allowed or not, your child will still bring the attachments that he or she has to previous caregivers, family members, and all of the children in all of the homes where s/he has previously lived. Your family may suddenly be MUCH larger than you expect.*

■■■

Our first family celebration after Shane's arrival was a little more complicated than I anticipated. Suddenly, I didn't just have my own family to include, but all of his as well. It was a big group.

The occasion was an official welcoming and commitment ceremony that took place at the church we attended. It was in some ways like a wedding, except that the promises were all one-sided – I made promises, Shane giggled. Virtually everyone Shane knew and loved was invited, along with all the members of his new family-to-be. That meant that when we ate together afterwards, around the tables sat his new adoptive family, his biological siblings, their adoptive families, the additional children those families had adopted or were currently fostering, as well as a few previous foster brothers and sisters and *their* families. There were people everywhere, eating on chairs in the kitchen, the sanctuary, the meeting rooms, and in the halls.

In the few months he had been with us, I had learned that not only were his *biological* brothers and sisters his brothers and sisters, but also all of *their* biological, foster and adopted brothers and sisters; his *former* foster brothers and foster sisters were his brothers and sisters along with all of *their* biological and adoptive siblings and former foster brothers and foster sisters. Since he had lived in twenty-one different placements before he came to live with us, he also had twenty-one sets of foster parents, foster grandparents, aunts, uncles, cousins, and staff members, all of whom he considered members of his family. You may think a child waiting for adoption has no family of their own at all, and sometimes you may be right, but more than likely, you just have NO IDEA!

••

Consider…

What information do you need in order to make good decisions about who to allow continued contact with, and how much contact to permit? Who can help you make these decisions?

Whom does it make sense to let your adopted child see regularly? Occasionally? Rarely? Never? What if the agency makes a decision about your foster child that you think is not in your child's best interest?

How is your immediate family likely to respond to this kind of complicated family constellation? Are you ready to accept it if your child refers to any number of other people as "Mom" or "Dad" and loves them, too?

How will your parents and extended family members take it if your child/ren have other people they are already related to as grandparents, aunts, uncles, and cousins? When members of your current family are trying to bond with this new child, how will they be affected by his/her attachment to others, both previous and subsequent to their involvement? Will all those people be welcome at your table, too?

❧ NOTES ☙

6. Physicians

The Vampire Lady in Andersonland

Having a good physician lined up before the child arrives is imperative, whether a family practitioner or a pediatrician (depending on the size of the city in which you live). Your agency may have a list of physicians they either require (in the case of foster children) or recommend. Since most older children waiting for placement will have been abused at some point in their lives, either by their birth family, foster families, or the system that is supposed to be protecting them, the physician should be well versed in the symptoms and effects of abuse, and how to deal with it in children. If that is not possible, s/he needs to be willing to learn, and to be very patient with a child who may be reluctant, if not unwilling, to be touched or examined by any health care provider. Treating such children can be a challenge for even the most experienced of physicians!

Our family had been going to the same General Practitioner for about fifteen years before Shane came along. That was then, of course, where we took Shane for his adoption physical just after he arrived.

It was not an easy visit. The first part of the exam was uneventful enough, but it is hard to do an exam on a child who has been as badly abused as Shane had been. When he was asked for a urine sample, for instance, he proceeded to do his best to tear Examination Room #1 apart.

Dr. Anderson and his nursing staff took it all in stride. Although in years to come Shane would grow to love "the Vampire Lady" who draws his blood, that was not the case on his first visit. We discussed taking him to the hospital and strapping him to a gurney to get a blood sample, but in the end, we just skipped that part of the exam altogether. There are days and times when things just aren't worth the effort.

Years later, Dr. Anderson is now talking about retiring, and I dread the day – because Shane still doesn't want to let anyone else touch him. He has already declared his intention to follow Charlotte the Vampire Lady wherever she goes. Maybe, if I am lucky, Dr. Anderson is just joking. But I don't think so.

Consider…

What health care providers for children are available in the community in which you live?

Interview the most likely physician candidates before the arrival of your child/ren in order to determine their experience and/or willingness to work with young people who have been emotionally, physically, or sexually abused.

Choose one with a sense of humor, if possible. S/he will need it, and so will you and your child. You have no way to appreciate yet just how handy the ability to laugh will be in the years to come. Parent one of these children, and you soon will.

NOTES

7. Therapists

Pre-Shrink, Shrink, Shrank, Shrunk

*Another person your child will need is a good therapist. This is not a commentary on your ability to parent a child with problems; it is just the truth. The incident rate for virtually every conceivable mental illness goes up in this population, primarily due to the disruption of the child's bond with his or her birth parents. Not long ago, there was a memorable day at our local adolescent psychiatric unit when the staff realized that 100% of the youngsters on the unit that day were adopted. That doesn't mean your child necessarily **will** have psychiatric problems, but the odds are pretty high. Your child will need someone s/he can talk to about you and the feelings that arise about being fostered/adopted, about their birth parents and their feelings about being abandoned, and to whom they can complain about how "their **real** parents would have let them do that." S/he will also need to have an outlet to talk about issues of abuse, confusion of loyalty, and a million other things that a birth child might not necessarily need a therapist for, but an abandoned child will.*

Depending on the resources available in your community, you may have virtually untrained counselors, a public mental health center, master's level therapists, or doctors (either psychiatrists [doctors with an M.D. who specialize psychiatry] or psychologists [doctors with a Ph.D. who specialize in psychology]) available in private practice. Whoever you choose, it will be helpful to have them lined up before a child ever comes to you, and to start the child in therapy immediately upon arrival. This will get your child/ren into the habit of going on a regular basis before a crisis makes it unavoidable – and it may make it possible to circumvent an emergency or two in the process.

Make sure you pick a practitioner you have interviewed in advance, and have reason to believe will be someone you can work with over the long haul. If possible, pick someone who has been in practice for a while, and who intends to stay in your community for the foreseeable future. Longevity in physical and mental health care providers is definitely a plus. Changing providers will likely prove to be extremely difficult, both for you and for your child. Your child/ren will probably need to be in therapy for a long time before trust develops, and your child's therapist can become your best advocate with a difficult system, as well as with your child.

••

Shane was lucky enough to be adopted by a family that already had a really great doctor – to whom we fondly refer as our Shrink – although Shane in particular has long debated whether or not he shrinks our heads, our wallets, or our problems. (In case you're wondering, that makes pre-shrinks therapists with less than a doctor's degree. If you've been to see one, you've been shrunk.) Noel and I had already been going to the same psychologist for years (even before Shane came along) because it kept us more or less sane, and also because it made it possible for us to live well with each other. Shane, however, was not sure he was willing to buy into that relationship.

I first met Doc when I worked for the CASA program out of the local juvenile court. That is also where I first came into contact with Shane's family, as he and all the other kids in his extended family had CASAs. Doc was the doctor you wanted to get for your client if you represented a child who was gravely wounded. As far as I knew, he was regarded as the best doctor in town to get for the most complicated cases. So of course, when I wanted a psychotherapist for my own kids whom I found to be pretty complicated, he was my first choice. He was not, however, Shane's first choice.

It's hard to imagine exactly what Shane's first choice would have been like, since he was completely unable to put any feelings – other than rage – into words. In fact, it was many years before we celebrated the realization that Shane had experienced a feeling and had told us about it on the same day. He was, however, able to make it perfectly clear to us that Doc was not *any* of his choices, not even the last. Shane didn't like talking, he didn't like feelings, and he especially didn't like men. He was terrified of men. And, if he had anything to do with it, he was *not* going to be in an office with one.

For more than two years, at least twice every week Shane would refuse to go in to the office. When that would happen, Doc would go out to talk with him in the parking lot. They would have what we came to call "Parking Lot Therapy." Frequently, Doc would have to get into the car with him, or less frequently, stand outside the car and talk to him through the window on those rare occasions when Shane was able to lock us both out. Eventually, Shane got to the point that, while he did not yet trust Doc enough to be in a room with him, he would go for walks with him. Together they would walk up and down the block while Shane would alternately hang on Doc and try to hurt him.

After a while, we graduated to "McDonald's Therapy," as in the "If you'll come into the office for part of the session this time, then next time we'll meet at McDonald's" method. It was therapy like I had never seen it done before. But then, I'd never met anyone as badly wounded as Shane before, either.

On one particularly notable occasion, Shane and I were outside in the car in the parking lot and I was unable to go in to tell them we were there because Shane was so out of control. He was hitting me in the back of the head over the back of the seat, and screaming. I was trying desperately to somehow protect myself without hurting him, and while I was doing a fair job of not hurting him, I was doing a miserable job of protecting myself.

When we didn't show up inside, Doc came out to look for us. With Doc's help, the two of us together were able to get hold of Shane's arms and legs, which helped minimize the damage he was doing to me, but we made no attempt to control his mouth. Shane continued to scream at the top of his lungs, "I can't breathe," and one of my all-time favorites, "The blood is rushing to my head." I never was too sure what it meant, but he used to say it all the time. Then, when he realized he couldn't hit us anymore, he started spitting. Quickly, Doc's shirt and face became covered in spit as he continued to talk quietly to Shane in an attempt to get him to calm down.

At some point during this exchange (with two adults struggling to hold down a screaming child) someone came out to a car in the adjoining parking lot, assumed that Doc and I were abusing Shane, and called the police. By the time the police officer arrived, Shane had calmed down sufficiently that we had been able to get him into the office, so that is where we were when the officer came in. The exchange between the officer and Shane started off like this:

"Are you hurt?"

Shane, nodding: "Yes."

"Where?"

Shane, lip quivering: "On my arm."

"Can you show me?"

Shane, sniffling: "Yes. There."

"I don't see anything. How did your arm get hurt?"

Shane, pointing: "He was holding me."

"Why was he holding you?"

Shane, wailing: "I was hitting my mother."

By the time the officer left, he was saying to Shane, "I really think you ought to try talking to this guy (Doc) some more. I think he can help you." Thank goodness, Shane has always been an honest child. He may not always understand exactly what is going on, and he frequently tells you he's NOT going to talk about something. But if he tells you he believes something happened, you could bank on it that he is telling you what he honestly believes. Otherwise, I guess I'd be writing this from jail.

•••

Consider…

Find out in advance if your child's mental health provider will need to be chosen from a list given to you by the state or agency who has the child in care, *and* if the provider must accept the state insurance plan or yours.

If your child/ren will need medication monitoring, make sure your find a psychiatrist (an M.D. who specializes in psychiatric treatment and medication) in addition to someone who specializes in talk therapy. Most other medical practitioners are unprepared to monitor psychotropic medications unless they have been trained specifically to do so.

As you interview candidates, ask if they are licensed, what they studied and where, and what their experience has been with **foster/adopted/special-needs children.**

When you interview potential mental health providers, keep in mind that you will probably be working with them for years. Choose someone who is likely to be able to provide that sort of long-term support. Choose someone with a sense of humor (you're going to need it) and choose someone who has a large repertoire of concrete, helpful ideas. In a counselor, you want someone who not only knows how to talk to kids and how to listen to them, but also knows things such as the best hold for a raging child. (My personal favorite, which may or may not work for you and your child/ren, was sitting on the floor with a padded couch behind me, holding the child in my lap with his back towards me, my legs crossed over his, his arms crossed in front of him with my hands holding his opposite hand on either side of his waist, and leaning forward with my head as close as possible to his. That way, I didn't have to worry about falling off a chair, the back of my head was padded in case I got rammed backwards into the wall – which unfortunately happened frequently – my legs held down the child's legs making it harder for him to either kick me or escape, my arms were not in front of him so I didn't get bitten quite so often, and with my head close to his, he couldn't get enough momentum to really hurt me when he smashed into my face with the back of his skull.) Someone who knows that kind of thing is the person you are looking for.

When you find one you think you can work with, be prepared for your child to be quite possibly less than grateful for your choice.

NOTES

8. Legalities

Contracts and Expectations

Typically, a foster care contract will be signed at the time of placement, delineating legal and financial responsibilities for each of the parties, as well as conditions for termination of the agreement. In contrast, you may (or may not) have a few months after a child arrives to finalize an Adoption Assistance contract, because adopted children usually have to be in a home for six months to a year before their adoption is final. These contracts concern federal adoption subsidies administered by individual states, which are available to families adopting children considered hard-to-place. Included are children who are older, have handicapping conditions, or constitute a sibling group. ASK if your child/ren qualify, and if so, what the timeline for the contract will be.

In addition to a financial subsidy and basic health insurance benefits, it is possible to write into Adoption Assistance contracts coverage for specific needs above and beyond the norm, such as higher board rates, respite, and medical coverage in excess of that offered by the government insurance policy. However, before these extraordinary provisions can be written into a contract, some states require certification **prior to adoption** that a hard-to-place child is in another, more specific, category of need, and **only** if that is done can special coverage be included. MAKE SURE you find out from your agency if any type of certification is necessary **before** you sign the contract. Afterwards it will be too late, and depending on the child, this may be very important. My own adopted children, for instance, typically exhausted their standard insurance coverage for each calendar year under both our family policy and their state policy sometime around the end of February. Without the additional services written into their Adoption Assistance contracts, they would have had no coverage at all for about ten months out of every year.

If you are adopting a special-needs child who qualifies for an adoption subsidy, you will need to have the child examined by competent medical, psychological, educational and social service personnel. You will want each of those providers to evaluate the child and to give you **in writing** an idea of the services you need to anticipate and write into the initial contract. GET WRITTEN RECOMMENDATIONS from each of them regarding both the probable – and the maximum – needs your child is likely to have prior to the age of twenty-one. These needs **must** be documented before the contract is signed in order for them to be covered.

You will also want to MAKE SURE the contract provides maximum benefits for both medical and psychotherapeutic services, even if you hope never to take advantage of these services. This is the time to think ahead. Will a wheelchair be needed at any time in the future? How about a handicap-accessible van? If you are adopting an infant who was born after prenatal exposure to drugs or alcohol, what about treatment for alcohol and drug addiction further down the line? MAKE SURE you include family therapy in addition to individual therapy. Some things may be partially covered by insurance, but others will need to be specifically itemized in the contract itself.

While adoption contracts can sometimes be amended later, they typically **cannot** be changed later to include provision for any service **unless** it was documented at the time of the child's placement that the condition was "pre-existing." YOU WILL undoubtedly have to supply the state with copies of the written evaluations in order to ensure that these services are written into the contract. INCLUDING a maximum benefit of 365 days of psychiatric hospitalization a year is an excellent idea. If you don't need it, great; if you do need it, it will be covered. But just putting hospitalization in the contract is not enough. MAKE SURE you have written into the contract a provision for **residential** treatment **and day** treatment. You can be sure that if *the only coverage listed is for hospitalization, it will be argued that the state is not liable for a lesser level of care, even if it is less expensive and all your child's providers agree that residential treatment is required. Your contract needs to SPECIFY that this may include wilderness programs, therapeutic daycare, respite, emergency foster care, and residential treatment programs. This will be **crucially** important later, if your child ever actually needs that level of service.*

For years, I fought with the State on an almost daily basis in order to get my children the services they had been guaranteed at the time of their adoptions. It was too bad I couldn't get paid for it. It was practically a full-time job.

One day, when I was at the Center for Adoption to deliver an appeal about their refusal of a treatment that Shane needed – even though it was less expensive than one we had anticipated and had written into the contract – the Director of Adoptions told me I needed to carry the form over to another office. Not sure of the protocol, I asked if I would need to tell them who I was when I dropped it off, or if I just handed it to the person at the desk.

"Oh, you don't have to tell them who you are. They *all* know you down there! You're *notorious*!" was the reply.

Thinking it had something to do with the fact that she had frequently suggested that I "just needed to adopt some of their more normal children," I joked, "Why is that? Because I only take children no one in their right mind would take?"

"Oh, no," the director laughed. "It's because *you* expect services for them *after* you get them."

Consider...

Before you agree to accept a child – while it's not too late to change your mind – think about the types of children you are willing to parent. Interview other caregivers of these types of children, if possible. Then list every single possibility you can imagine of every type of care they might ever need.

Now that you've made your list, think about the ramifications of each type of care. What would it mean to you? To your spouse? To your family? To your other relationships?

Does this make a difference in the type of child you are willing to consider? Do you need to revise your previous list of criteria of acceptable conditions?

Now, find a good attorney who can read over your contract for you when the time comes.

NOTES

9. SELF CARE

Heal Me, Please

*Your child is not the only one who will need support; you may end up needing more assistance than you ever imagined could be necessary. In this respect, receiving a child is just like giving birth. You simply cannot anticipate every need that will arise, and taking care of yourself is of major importance if a placement is going to work in the long run. Unless **you** are cared for, you will not be able to offer your child whatever it is s/he needs. If you are a couple, you need to schedule time alone together, at all costs. You will **have** to tend to your own relationship first before either of you will be able to care for anyone else. You can be sure that if the two of you don't get the time you need together, your child will act as a barometer of the tension that the family is experiencing. If you are feeling tense, s/he will act it out! Your failure to care for yourselves will exacerbate your child's needs for care. If you want your family to survive, make your plans for self care now.*

Shane had only been with me a few weeks when in desperation I called my friend Deborah, and asked for a massage. When she got a look at me, she was appalled. I was already covered with bruises, and my arms were raw from the bites. I stayed that way for years.

Compassionately, she took us on as a project, and decided she could best help Shane by ministering to me. Until she moved a couple of years later, she would weekly massage and work over my wounded body so that I could go back and take Shane's abuse for another week. She never charged me a thing for the service. For a while, after several tutors had quit and I was desperate, she even tutored Shane as together we tried to tame him.

Years later, when Deborah moved to Florida to care for her mother and grandmother, Bonnie took over the job of trying to heal my body so that I could try to heal Shane's soul. I would never have made it without them.

Consider…

What provision does your agency make for respite if either adoptive/foster parents or the children themselves need it?

Find out if it is possible to write coverage into your contract for the medical damage your child may do to you or the physical damage s/he may do to your home or possessions.

Ask about the agency's procedure for paying for respite services. Sometimes the state where I live is in excess of two years behind on paying providers, and I have had several quit for that reason. Make sure you have an attorney consider what happens if respite providers are not paid in a timely manner. You're *not* going to want providers to quit because of untimely payment. You *are* going to need them.

What can you anticipate needing that will help you support the relationships you already have in place?

What *other* support services for yourselves can you put into place before your child/ren arrive?

What provisions can you make for time alone (and if a couple, for time alone together) without children?

Line up several babysitters in advance that you can call when the time comes. Do it now, while you still have the time.

ꙮ NOTES ꙮ

10. Anger

What's That You Say?

Many times, issues that have deeply impacted our child/ren are hard for us to take seriously. Sometimes, that is because things that are of major importance to children seem insignificant to us given our perspective of being older and having lived longer. Other times, with fostered/adopted children as well as with birth children, even if we know something is important to them it is hard not to laugh because what kids say is just so, well, funny.

*Children are excruciatingly sensitive to being laughed at, and their sensitivity is amplified when they are angry. And they **are** going to get angry with you, just as you are going to get angry with them. They will be angry because you must set limits. They will be angry because you are acting like a parent. They will be angry because you are fostering or adopting them, and they'll be angry because you're not their "real" parent, even though frequently that's who they're really angry with but just can't say so.*

*We can respond by reflecting what they say or mean, "You're really mad at me." We can respond by letting them know they have been heard, "You don't think it is fair that you can't go." We can respond by telling them how their words have made us feel, "I feel sad that you are upset, **and** I still am unwilling to let you go." (The **and** is very important. If you use **but** it effectively negates everything you just finished saying.) Sometimes, though, the best we can do is to respond to them as literally as they speak, completely ignoring the connotations that our age and perspective give us. Intended slurs that are meant personally can be responded to as explanations of figures of speech, without ever addressing the underlying insult. But you can always tell your friends and laugh about it later, when your child/ren can't hear what you are saying!*

Prior to Shane's being taken into the custody of the state, he was almost deaf due to repeated ear infections. Although he could hear a little, he did not hear well at all. His language skills were impaired as a result, and he had such difficulty speaking that it was hard for most folks to understand him.

In spite of that, he wanted desperately to go to daycare. Social workers were able to get him enrolled, but have told me stories of Shane as a four-year-old, dressing himself and standing next to the door, crying when the bus from the speech and hearing center would come to get him because no one inside the house would get up to open the door to let him out. The times he was able to get there, however, were time well spent. Shane learned to sign. Unfortunately, he didn't learn to spell.

He learned that in most settings he could curse in sign and get away with it, so for a long time after I got him, he would sign furiously whenever he got mad. The difficult part as a parent was not to laugh when he firstly used curse words entirely wrongly, and secondly spelled them hysterically inaccurately. He couldn't hear well and couldn't speak clearly, so he was just guessing at what he was spelling. It was, as my friend Nancy says, a hoot.

After he was placed into state custody, tubes were put in his ears and his hearing improved, but it was years before he could consistently speak so that others could understand what he said. Although on the one hand his mistakes were often funny, on the other hand it must have been excruciatingly frustrating for him to have people constantly asking, "What? Could you say that again? I'm sorry, Shane. I just do not understand what you are saying."

Eventually, he got to the point that he would curse out loud when he was mad, but he still used the words all wrong. We would try not to laugh, and I would infuriate him when I calmly said things like, "Shane, I can't be what you said I am. I am not a son of anything at all. I am a daughter."

If he is mean to me when I am old and helpless, I will probably have earned it.

• •

Consider…

You can expect your children to get angry with their circumstances, with others, and with you, whether you think you deserve it or not. Make a plan in advance for how to respond. What are acceptable ways of addressing and expressing anger in your family? Write them down and post them on the refrigerator door; go over the list whenever the issue arises. Ask your children for suggestions of things you can add. One such list might contain suggestions such as "say who you are angry with and why," "hit the couch pillows," "tear up old phone books," "stomp on the stuffed green frog," and "break the glass bottles for recycling." Make sure you wear safety goggles if you include the last one. It works best if you throw the bottles into those big metal recycling containers because the crash makes an exceptionally great sound, but there is always the possibility that the glass will fly!

What ways was anger expressed in your family of origin?

Which of those ways were positive, and which were negative?

Which ones do you want to hold on to? Which ones would be better to let go of?

Make a list of fair fighting rules, and insist that your child/ren respect it. Set for them the example of following it yourself.

Save your laughter for your partner, spouse, or friends when you are certain your children will not be able to overhear you. Someday, your children may be able to laugh with you, but it will not likely be for a very long time.

NOTES

11. Rejection

"I'm biting your motherrrr!"

Adopted and fostered children have typically been rejected many times before they ever get to you. They have been torn from birth families, and rejected by foster families. They have repeatedly lost communities, extended families, and friends. As a result, they are likely to fear that as soon as they get attached to you, you will reject them and they will lose you, too.

Typically, then, they try to get it over with as soon as possible. After a short honeymoon, which they cannot maintain forever, children will become as obnoxious as possible. "Go ahead and get rid of me," they dare you. "Get it over with." Sometimes they will use words, but more often they will act it out. Their fear, of course, is that the longer it takes and the more attached to you they become, the more painful the loss will be when it happens. Expect this stage. Take it in stride. If you can ride it out, there is hope on the other side. But be warned that the length of this stage will correspond to the length of time they spent in other homes before coming to you. The older they are and the more they have been moved around, the longer it will take for them to feel safe with you.

It may seem at the time like this stage is lasting forever, but it will not, though it could take several years. Trust takes time to develop. The flip side is that the blossoming you will see once you have earned it is worth every minute you invested.

• •

I first met Shane on the day before his 10th birthday. He was a tiny little boy. Having had Failure to Thrive, he was, at ten years old, smaller than all but two of the seven-year-olds in his second grade classroom. He was short for his age, and frighteningly thin. He made up for his size, however, in strength.

During his daily rages, which would happen every time his Posttraumatic Stress Disorder (PTSD) was triggered, he put out so much effort struggling that it was all I could do to keep him from destroying the house along with me. While I would struggle to get him into the holds our doctor had taught me, he would do as much damage as he possibly could. Frequently, he would be screaming at his abusers, for that was who he saw in his mind's eye, and from whom he was trying to protect himself.

Almost anything could set him off, and it was many years before I learned enough of his triggers that we could have an even halfway normal life. Even having the wrong kind of breakfast cereal could remind him of something horrible that had happened to him, to say nothing of the trauma of going to the doctor.

He could not tolerate change. He was terrified of the unknown. We would have to go over the schedule for each day over and over again to try to reassure him and prepare him for whatever lay ahead. In addition, he thought that (like all his other mothers) I would make him leave, and he was determined to get it over with as soon as possible.

One day in particular, something long since forgotten happened which triggered him, and I was once again trying to hold him down to contain his anger until he had worn himself out. It was a process which could take as long as two hours, and on really bad days, could happen as many as three times in a day. That day I was lying on top of him, trying once more to get him into a hold, when he bit clean through the sweatshirt I was wearing. Blood started pouring from the wound. Within minutes my sweatshirt was soaked with scarlet.

When he saw it, I could almost see the wheels turning in his head as he thought of a new way to manipulate us into wanting to get rid of him. "Neaow, Neaow!!!" he started calling. Only when Noel got to the door of the room and could see what he had done, did he start yelling, "Ah'm bitiiin' youahr muvvahh!"

••

Consider…

What has your child/ren's history been prior to arriving at your home? How many times have they been moved, and over what time span?

Think back to times you have been betrayed. How long did it take you to recover, to trust again? How old were you when it happened? How much experience did you have with others who were trustworthy? Those variables affected the length of your recovery. Expect that to be true for your child/ren as well.

Anticipating that your child/ren will attempt to drive you away, what can sustain you in your commitment to them? What bearing does your faith have on your commitment to others? How does your understanding of the steadfastness of God and/or your parental figures impact your expectation of steadfastness in yourself?

What can you do to facilitate forgiving yourself when your patience wears unbearably thin?

How can you get the respite you need to give yourself a break before going back and trying again?

❧ NOTES ☙

12. Compassion

Moses

Empathy for others' feelings is a difficult skill for anyone to learn, but for children who have been repeatedly moved from one caregiver to another, it can be even more challenging. It is hard to learn to read the feelings of others when too little time is allowed to develop relationships with them.

In spite of that, even young children can be encouraged to imagine others' feelings. Asking questions such as "How would you feel if that happened to you?" or making statements like, "If that happened to me, I'd feel…" can help them to learn to recognize not only others' feelings, but their own. Children who have difficulty recognizing their impact on the world around them can be helped by your use of the phrase "When you _____, I feel _____." While it is not necessary for children to divest themselves of their possessions, they can be encouraged to share with their playmates with words such as, "She might like to play, too." Any time children see beyond their own needs to the needs of others is a gift in and of itself.

During those moments when Shane's PTSD was not being triggered by one thing or another, he was the most generous child I knew. He especially loved giving to people who were more helpless and more powerless than he was. This included both people who were very old and children who were even younger than he. There was nothing he would keep from someone who needed anything he could offer, if it was within his power to give it to them.

He would literally give away his clothes, his toys, or his money. He would do any kind of manual labor anyone needed done, and because of his great strength, there were lots of things he could do. But his favorite thing to do was to care for others in kind and gentle ways. He would search out anything anyone asked for. He would help anyone do absolutely anything they wanted help with. And he could put up with things that drove many of the rest of us crazy.

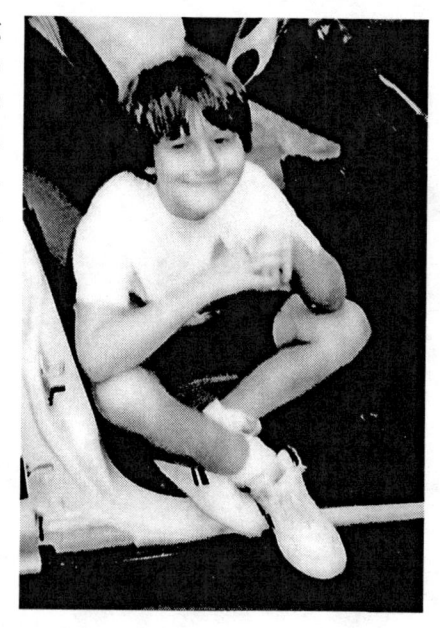

Moses was a case in point. Younger than Shane and multiply handicapped, he was named for another friend of ours who Shane absolutely adored. Part of that adoration carried over to the young namesake, but that did not explain all of Shane's affinity for young Moses. It was as though Shane recognized in Moses someone more needy than himself, and knowing what it was like to suffer, he wanted to help ease others' suffering in any way he could.

Moses, for his part, could be excruciatingly frustrating for his Sunday School teachers and their aides. Once he learned to walk, he was constantly trying to escape from his classroom. During worship he could be disruptive, and when it was time for the children to go to Children's Church during the sermon it would take him a exceedingly long time to walk out of the sanctuary, so that all the other children had to wait. But no matter how frustrating he was, Shane never lost patience with him.

As Shane gained in confidence, he slowly took it upon himself to be Moses' helper. He would ever so slowly and patiently guide Moses out of the sanctuary, sit with him during children's activities, and entertain him when he would get disruptive. It was a role Shane seemed comfortable in, and we knew he must have played the same sort of role in his birth family trying to care for his younger sister and twin brothers, who he continued to miss desperately.

Although over the years Shane would take on this helper role with many others, Moses was always one of his favorites, and remains so to this day.

....

Consider...

How can you find ways to cultivate the positive relationship skills your child/ren *did* develop in their families of origin? (You may have to look for them.)

What relationships with other adults can you help develop for your child/ren so that they learn to look beyond their own needs to the needs of others?

Which playmates can you make opportunities for your child/ren to play with to give them exposure to other children with needs greater than their own?

❧ NOTES ☙

13. PLAY

Possum Stew

As children learn about the world around them, they frequently "play out" what is going on inside their heads. As a result, play therapy is a common technique among many therapists who use children's instinctive use of play to their benefit. Given a palate of toys from which to choose, much can be learned about the internal goings-on of children's thinking by watching what they do with the toys available to them.

Therapists are not the only ones who can use this technique to learn about your children. If you will pay attention to the games your children play, you can usually piece together the things that worry them and help them make sense of their play at the same time. Sometimes, the thoughts they play out will be obvious on the surface, as children attempt to gain mastery over the things they are worried about. Other times, you can pick up on themes in your children's thinking.

Any concerns that you have need to be brought to the attention of the child's therapist; but frequently, as you become aware of fears, you can comfort the child yourself. Perhaps the most valuable thing you can do, however, is just to give your child the words for what s/he is already acting out. "That dinosaur is really roaring!" "The daddy doll is hitting the mommy." "The big horse is protecting the little one." On occasion, you can also suggest different possible endings than the ones your children have thought of already. Sometimes, though, as in this example, children arrive at satisfactory endings all by themselves!

Occasionally, we would see a possum in our backyard, even though we lived right in the midst of the city. As far as we could tell, it was living under a storage building we had, and just every once in a while it would appear at dusk so that we got a glimpse of it. It would terrify Shane. Finally, he got to the point that he did not like going into the backyard by himself at all, even in broad daylight. One day, however, as I was in the kitchen cooking lunch, he ventured out into the yard on his own.

From the window, I could see him carefully collecting bricks and putting them into a circle. He made a pile of sticks and gathered rocks, and put them by the bricks. Finally, he came into the kitchen asking for a large pot. "Sure," I replied, and got him one. With some amusement, I asked, "What'cha making?"

"Possum Stew," he very seriously replied, and went back out. He continued with the ritual of placing all the items he had collected into the pot, pretending to light the fire, pretending to cook, taste, and season the stew, and then finally pretending to eat it all up. Having gained mastery over the possum in play, from that day on he was never afraid of the possum in the yard again.

Consider…

What themes do you notice arising time and again in your child/ren's play?

What concerns or fears do these themes suggest that your child/ren are experiencing?

Can you put words to your child/ren's feelings for them? "That doll is really acting angry!" "This elephant feels scared and mad when you hit it with that one." They may have the actions to express their feelings, but you can supply them with the words they need to help them think.

Imagine you are your child. After s/he has played out his or her own ending to the scenario being acted out, how is s/he likely to feel? What would you like to have happened? What ending would you like that play to have? Can you suggest it to your child? Can you model it for him or her?

With whom can your child play to help fill the gaping holes left by the losses already experienced?

ℬ NOTES ☙

14. Discernment

Twiko

All children, in their innocence, suffer from what occasionally looks to adults like poor judgment. They misjudge information and misinterpret data. Their projections of anticipated results are faulty. Everything they see and hear goes through the filter of their interpretation of things they have seen and heard before.

What looks to us like bad judgment is sometimes actually good judgment based on too little information, whether we can understand the logic or not. Depending on the circumstances of a child's past experiences, children's interpretations of current facts can sometimes lead to disastrous results. More frequently, though, near-disasters are averted. As one of my friends says, maybe there really is a separate God just to watch over children. I know mine sure need it.

Ingrid and her brother, Lee, inherited their mother's dog when she died. Tiko was quite possibly the second most obnoxious dog I had ever known. Ingrid and Lee were stuck with him, however, because they did not believe they could get rid of their deceased mother's dog. Short and hairy, his most notable trait was that he bit everyone he met, for any reason at all. The most commonly experienced of those reasons was that he hated haircuts, and anyone who tried to give him one was mincemeat. As a consequence, whenever he needed one (which was far too often), he had to be taken to the vet and sedated.

Shane, for his part, has never been able to recognize when animals don't like him. Although he assumes all people are dangerous, for some reason he believes and acts as though all animals love him. And he knew that night that Tiko, who must have loved him, couldn't see and needed a haircut. When Ingrid and Lee stepped outside for a few minutes, he did what almost any kid would do. He headed immediately for the scissors and the dog.

By the time Ingrid and Lee came back inside, Shane and Tiko were on the couch, which was covered with hair. Shane, with scissors in hand, looked seriously at Ingrid, and said, "Ingwid, I gave Twiko a haiwcut." Why the dog hadn't killed him, we never understood.

Consider…

What kinds of dangers lurk around your home for an unsuspecting child?

Just as it is a good idea for a family to have a fire escape plan, it is also a good idea to think through responses to other disasters. Talk with your child/ren about what constitutes an emergency (life threatening) versus a non-emergency. What plans can you put in place for dealing with the various scenarios?

Talk aloud with your child as you go through your own decision making process. Let him/her hear the steps you go through. S/he can get an idea about how to interpret dangerous data or to avert disaster by listening to you make plans of your own.

Talk with your child/ren about the people you consider it safe to be around, and why. Help him/her to talk about people and animals s/he knows. What makes each of them dangerous or safe? Why? How do they need to be responded to differently, depending on the answer?

NOTES

15. FORGIVENESS

This Time It Wasn't the Cat that Ate the Canary!

There are times in all of our lives when, by carelessness, oversight, or on purpose, we participate in activities that grieve those we love. When our children take part in such an activity that affects us, it has the potential to be either destructive or life giving. Our most human response at such times is to blame anyone handy for our grief, no matter what the age of the instigator. Controlling that instinct is one of the most powerful tools we have at our disposal as parents.

Thinking back on your life, is it the times you were raked over the coals that made the greatest impact on your life, or was it the times you were undeservedly forgiven? Most of us remember punishment with resentment and fear. Typically, forgiveness prompted us to try to act in such a way as to deserve it. That will usually be true for our children, too.

One year, on my birthday, Shane found a puppy in the yard. Tiny little black puppy, it was exuberant and full of life. Bouncing, running, leaping, licking, it was a bundle of joy, and was itself delighted to have been found. It was a perfect match for my endlessly moving bundle of boy. Climbing, laughing, eating, talking, Shane was full of non-stop excitement at his glorious find. He could hardly stop playing with it long enough to come in and tell me about what it was doing now, before he had to rush back outside and play with it some more. In and out and in and out of the house again, the way children tend to do, he was having so much fun I could hardly contain my own joy at what a happy, normal way it was for a small boy to spend the day.

We were at home that morning beginning the early stages of my favorite way to celebrate my birthday, because my ritual birthday celebration all my adult life had been to put up and decorate my Christmas tree. I loved all the parts involved in that celebration: the cleaning of the house, the annual rearranging of the furniture so the tree would fit in the corner by the window where my reading chair usually sat. I especially loved going out with the kids to pick out the tree when they got home from school, and decorating the tree that night with all the ornaments which had been gifts over the years. Each ornament stood for someone who had loved me, at some particular point in my life. Although there were a few whose origin I had forgotten, even those were special because they had come to represent all those who had been a part of my life at one time or another, and who had themselves been forgotten. Whatever children were at home that year would be allowed to help decorate until they lost interest, and then once they had all fallen asleep, I would finish, as the children were safe in their beds and the fire burned in the fireplace. My birthday had truly become a day when all felt right in the world.

All morning, Shane had been playing with the little puppy in the backyard as I worked around the house, until finally it was time for me to shower so I could join Martha for lunch. Each year since the year I was exactly half her age, Martha and I have gone to eat lunch at one of the local bookstores during our birthday week. She has become almost a mother to me, and I almost a daughter to her. I was really looking forward to having our special birthday lunch with her again when I called Shane to come in the house so that I would know where he was while I showered. He came in, reluctant to leave the puppy outside, but he did come in.

Coming out of the shower, I was happy and pleased at what the rest of the day promised. Coming out of my room, I was thinking of all I had to look forward to. Coming down the stairs, I was anticipating dropping Shane off with a friend so that I could enjoy lunch with Martha. I did not, however, expect what I found at the bottom of the stairs: Shane, waiting to tell me that he had let the puppy in, and it had knocked the birdcage over. Ok, I thought, that's not too bad. I can fix that. It was not until I came into the dining room that I realized what the problem was. The bottom had separated from the cage, and the two lovebirds I had hand raised from fledglings were missing. With their wings clipped, they would not have been able to get very far, and Shane had not had any idea what to do. They were just gone. Completely gone.

I looked everywhere for them, but they were nowhere to be found. Only a few feathers remained of the birds I had spent several Christmases-Past watching. I had always enjoyed watching them climb over the branches of the tree, laughed at them playing with the bright ornaments, delighted in their eating the berries off the wreaths. Of the birds that I loved, only a few feathers remained, and a very full and happy puppy that had apparently devoured them both. The only relief I could find in their being eaten was in imagining the puppy's delight at finding a couple of throw toys who threw themselves. I may have been heartbroken, and Shane may have been afraid of what I might do, but the puppy must have thought it was really great fun.

....

Consider...

How do you decide on appropriate consequences for inappropriate behavior?

What is your most traumatic memory of punishment?

What is your most powerful memory of forgiveness?

Which way do you want to impact your child?

ಬಂ NOTES ಜಿ

16. Revelations

Holocaust

For adults, the question of self-disclosure is a difficult one. We are constantly trying to discern how much it is safe to tell someone else about ourselves. We try to gauge what the other person's reaction is likely to be to what we have to say. We worry about what someone else will think about us if they know certain things. And we have a lot more to base those judgments on than children do.

For some of the foster children who are waiting to be adopted or to go home, it is not just that self-disclosure might lead to rejection. Some children are rightfully afraid because telling others about what has gone on in the past could be life-threatening. It may be years before they can tell anyone else what happened to them, whether it is a teacher, friend, therapist, or you. This is NOT a reflection on you, your trustworthiness, or your love. It IS a reflection on the horror they experienced before they ever got to you. Asking what happened is likely to only put them on the spot and make them feel pressured to say something before they are ready. Frequently, demanding an answer will only cause them to shut completely down.

Instead, try to wait patiently until your child is ready to share. When something is disclosed, the best thing to do is to act as though there is absolutely nothing s/he could say that would surprise you, even if what you have just heard strikes terror in your heart and makes you physically ill. If your child knows that s/he has made you feel that way, all that will happen is that the next disclosure, if there is one, will be even longer in coming. Try to react calmly. Non-judgmentally, thank the child for telling you. Cry to someone else later if you have to, but never make your child feel responsible for your reaction. It may be more than s/he can bear.

The burden of evidence in juvenile court is different than in criminal court. It is possible to prove that children have been abused and remove them from the setting in which that abuse is taking place without necessarily being able to prove who perpetrated the abuse so that criminal charges can be filed. In Shane's family's case, the children were the only ones who could testify as to who abused them, but they had been so traumatized that for years if we even made the mistake of mentioning the abusers' names, Shane would vomit all over himself in fear. He would regularly take knives out of the kitchen and hide them all over the house because he feared he would have to defend himself if his abusers found out where he lived. These children would never have been able to testify in court, and their abusers never went to jail.

Still, on rare occasions, we would get glimpses of the horror that Shane had lived before he went into foster care. One day, Shane's tutor, Deborah, took him along with her daughter, Sarah, to see some exhibits at the Tennessee State Museum. Among the exhibits there that day was a Holocaust exhibit. Shane and Sarah were walking along looking at the pictures, and when they came to one photograph of piles of bodies stacked on top of each other, Shane matter-of-factly looked up at Deb and quietly said, "My _____ (and he named one of the relatives who had abused him) killed people."

Consider…

What is the worst thing you can imagine *your* child disclosing?

Suppose your child has just shared with you that the exact thing you just imagined either happened to him/her or was witnessed by him/her. If you were that child, how would you want the listener to react?

Now imagine that your child has just told you something even worse. You might want to make a list of terrible things that might possibly happen to people and pick something on the list more horrible than the one you chose above. *That's* the one you need to be ready for - the one that is even worse than you can readily envisage. If you can get ready for that one, then the one you are most likely to hear might be easier to bear.

What can you do to mentally prepare yourself to hear such a disclosure someday? You need to know that it can be agonizing to hear that something destructive happened to a child you have grown to love. Who will you call for support when the time comes?

Most states have child abuse reporting laws. Though what your child might disclose may be something that has already been reported, it also may not have been. Talk to the therapist you have chosen about how such a report is made, and who is required to make it.

You may not be able to erase what happened to your child, but you may be able to keep it from happening again, whether to your child or to someone else. That in and of itself can be empowering to you and to your child, too.

NOTES

17. FIDELITY

You Can Run, but You Cannot Hide

There is a wonderful little book out called "The Runaway Bunny" that tells of a mother's determination to hold on to a child of hers who wants to run away. While almost all children want to grow up and leave home someday, some of them can't wait that long. Some threaten to run away before they are grown, and some of them actually do so.

Physically holding on to children when they want to run away can be a powerful experience for both parents and children. We learn that even if we're exhausted afterwards we can in fact outlast them. And they learn a lesson birth children learned as infants – you are larger and more powerful than they are! In the short run outlasting them may be hard for you to pull off, especially the older and larger they are. In the long run, its lessons are crucially important for both of you to learn.

After Deborah left town to move to Florida, Ingrid took over as Shane's tutor. While Deborah had often focused on what she called "remedial childhood," even trying to teach Shane such basic skills as how to catch a ball, Ingrid had been a teacher for many years and focused on reading and math. They were both subjects Shane found incredibly difficult and painful. On Monday nights when I had to work late, Ingrid would come to my office and work with Shane in another area of the building while I met with my counseling clients.

One disastrous night, Shane decided he had suffered enough and ran out of the building in his shorts, leaving his shoes behind him. I was in my office and had no idea what was going on, while he took off down the street with Ingrid following him. All she could do was yell that he had better come back, because as she put it, she was "too old and fat" to catch him.

He had gotten about a half mile down the street, when just at that moment his psychiatrist, Jeri, came driving down the road on her way to the store. Jeri had already been Shane's doctor for a long time before I adopted him. He had been the very first patient to walk through her door, on the day she opened her first office, and had endeared himself to her by slamming her brand new desk chair into her brand new desk, permanently scarring them both. Okay, well, maybe not endeared. But he sure broke her in, in a way that bonded him to her dearly.

When Jeri first saw the small barefooted boy racing down the sidewalk her initial thought was, "Hmm, that little boy looks just like Shane," followed by, "It is Shane! I wonder what he's doing here all by himself." Jeri slowed her car and rolled the window down, trying to engage Shane in conversation as he sprinted down the sidewalk, going anywhere but tutoring as fast as he could. Eventually, she was able to talk him into getting into her car; she turned her car around and then drove him back to the office.

It was enough to convince him, for a little while at least, that he might be able to run away from us but he could not hide, because the people watching out for him were EVERYWHERE.

■■■

Consider…

While it is not really possible for any of us to be everywhere, it *is* possible for you to talk to your child about how determined you are not to let them go. Let your child tell you about the desire to run away without making any judgments. Hold on to the truth that most of your child's feelings are not a reflection on you. They are just your child's feelings.

If your child is willing to hear it, read aloud *The Runaway Bunny* or some other similar book. Talk with your child about feelings of wanting to run away. If your child is willing to listen, talk about times you have felt that way yourself.

Think about ways you can childproof your home to make it less likely that a child could successfully escape. Have photographs of your child/ren made on a regular basis so that you have a current photo if you need one. Many police departments will also fingerprint your child for an ID card if you so desire.

❧ NOTES ☙

18. GRIEF

Angela

Foster children have to deal with many losses while they wait for permanency, and the end of each relationship is like a death to them. Like the deaths we, too, have experienced, our children's losses are grieved for years. With multiple losses, each one exacerbates recovery from the losses that have gone before. Success at acceptance will be followed by relapse. Moving on will be intermingled with anger and despair. Thus, helping your child/ren deal with grief and death will be a constant part of your life for a long time after you have chosen to foster or adopt. As you grow to love the children who come to you, their losses will affect you, too.

The idea itself that a loss has occurred will take time to adjust to. Finding other sources of love and friendship to take the place of what is lost will take even longer, because with each loss the fear of loving again will be increased. A child's concept of death becomes intermingled with the concept of loss. Add the physical death of someone or something the child loves, and the equation becomes even more complicated.

My friend Angela was dying. She had no family in town other than her two-year-old son, Brandon, and eventually got to the point that she could no longer take care of herself. She wanted me to adopt Brandon, but at the time Shane needed so much attention that it was not realistic for me to make another commitment. We found another family delighted to adopt her sweet toddler, and Angela lovingly went through the process of slowly acclimating her beloved son to his new family.

A few weeks before her death, when her doctor anticipated that she did not have much longer to live, Brandon went to stay with the family that was going to adopt him. I signed up for enough vacation time to take care of her until she died, and Angela came home with me. For the last few weeks, Shane and I cared for her, until finally, at the very end, we had to take her back to the hospital after all. She hung on, determinedly, until her own physician came in to say goodbye, and then she died.

I was not in the room at the time, but Shane was, and he was taking it all in. When he realized she was gone, he started saying to himself and to my co-worker Vicki, who was also in the room, "She's a goner. Yep. She's a goner." He was still saying it over and over when I got back. There was not even a hint of disrespect, just a small child trying to understand his loss. "She's a goner. Yep. Angela's gone."

Consider...

Think back to losses you have had to face in the past. Did any occur when you were your child's age, or close to it? How did you resolve the loss?

Try to remember some period in your life when you had multiple losses within a short period of time. What was it like for you?

How old were you when you began to understand the concept of death? What helped make it more real for you?

What things did people say that were helpful to you at that time? It probably was not a platitude like, "They're in a better place," or "You'll get over it with time." Instead, what was it that *did* work to make you feel better? Was it something someone said, or something someone did?

How long did it take before you started to feel significantly better? How long was it before you felt safe in your relationships again?

What did it take for *you* to be willing to risk loving again?

NOTES

19. MOTIVATION

Eat Your Words

*When faced with goals that are too large or too far in the future, children are easily discouraged and are more likely to give up. This is especially an issue for children who have experienced multiple placements and do not have a history of longevity with anything or anyone to count on. Many of these children have found that in the end giving up is easier than dealing with the feelings connected with failure. At least if they quit they can tell themselves they **could** have done it if they had only tried harder or longer. Quitting does not feel quite as horrible as having failed.*

Whether it is with our friends or coworkers, adult family members or children, it is always difficult to know where to draw the line between supporting dreams and goals, and trying to be rooted in realism. We question whether we should be pushing, discouraging, or waiting. These issues become even more difficult when the goals are those of the special-needs child. Without the experience of small successes over time, foster and adopted children have no hope of being able to pull off large goals in the future. They almost always want to be "just like everyone else," but they simply aren't. They see other kids doing things they want to be able to do, but may not yet have the skills to pull off. Persistence is a luxury they have never been able to afford in the past. It is our job as their parents to help them get ready for possibilities of both success and failure, and to pick up the pieces (if need be) in order to help them move on.

*Encouraging your child/ren to hang in there with a task until it is attained can feel like an insurmountable goal, for the parent as well as the child. Sometimes it is all **we** can do to hold on for just one last try. The twelve-step mantra "One Day at a Time" can help, too, as can attendance at support groups such as the National Alliance of the Mentally Ill (NAMI). We can teach our children persistence by modeling it for them. We can keep encouraging them even when they want to give up. We can keep going ourselves even when WE want to give up. As Shane's doctor is always telling him, "The impossible just takes a little longer."*

• •

Poor Shane hated school with a passion, and tutoring was no better. In fact, anything having to do with academics was excruciatingly frustrating for him, because he just couldn't get it. He couldn't grasp even the simplest concepts, like sounding out letters and syllables or adding numbers together. The effort he put out was enormous, but it was never enough.

Ingrid kept patiently working with him anyway, using a set of cards on which words, numbers, and syllables were printed. One night, in desperation, he started eating the cards themselves. Ingrid had been trying to help him sound them out, and literally eating the words seemed to be the only way he could get the sounds in his mouth.

Ingrid, in an effort to save her cards, tried to wrestle them away from him, and Shane started to wrestle back. By the time I got there to pick him up, she was sitting on top of him (a pose I knew oh-so-well) and was trying to keep him from destroying her house as he had mine. He was screaming one of his favorite lines at the top of his lungs: "I can't breathe!"

Explaining to him that *of course* he was breathing, because he wouldn't have been able to *scream* unless he was breathing, had never helped any. All I could do was take him home, pray that she wouldn't quit on us, and hope that the next day would be a better day.

■ ●

Consider...

What ideas do you wrestle with that you can talk about to your child/ren, explaining that you, too, struggle with the issues of discouragement and hopelessness from time to time? Talk with your child/ren about what keeps you going at those times, and ask what might help them when they feel like giving up, too.

What support groups are available where you live from whom you might find encouragement to hang in there when it is your child/ren themselves that are wearing you out?

We all have to deal with disappointment. What do you do with yours? Is it turned into despair or self-degradation? Do you typically use what you learn from failures to motivate yourself to do better in the future? Which things that you tell yourself are helpful, and which ones hurt?

How can you use that information to motivate the child/ren you love?

NOTES

20. Guardian Angels

Sisyphus

Fighting the system on the behalf of foster and adopted children can feel to a parent like Sisyphus must have felt pushing that rock up that hill: you just know that once you get it up there someone will knock it down again. Contracts which promise to cover a child's pre-existing conditions (in the case of adoptions) or all of their needs (in the case of foster children) are painfully like that rock. They offer the promise of the top of the hill, but you spend all your time rock-pushing. Few parents are eager to give a child back in order to obtain promised services.

Typically, foster care contracts delineate fiscal and legal responsibility. In the case of adoptions, the contracts include a list of covered expenses the child is expected to need between the time of adoption and the age of either eighteen or twenty-one, depending on certain circumstances. This list might include medications, psychotherapy, organ transplant, hospitalization (either medical or psychiatric), respite, or other anticipated needs. Normally, only expenses which are anticipated at the time of the adoption are covered, since the rationalization is that if some unanticipated medical condition developed in one of your own birth children, you would have to be responsible for it. Only needs that you know the child has but are willing to take on anyway are covered by the adoption subsidy.

*If it really worked that way, it would be great. Unfortunately, the truth is that most contracts have an extra clause, which requires specific authorization in writing not just before any expenditure can be **covered**, but again before the expense is **incurred**. Therein lies the difficulty. If psychiatric hospitalization is covered, but you have to get state authorization before admission, what in the world are you going to do while you are waiting to get that authorization? You may not be able to maintain your child at home, but if you go ahead and admit the child to the hospital without written authorization, the state is relieved of their responsibility to pay. For the adoptive parent, it can be a no-win proposition.*

Frequently, the request for authorization is turned down automatically on first asking, even though a service has been written into the contract. In order to get approval, one must appeal up the ladder until – and if – the request finally reaches an administrator willing to approve it. States are not overly excited about paying for any service if they can argue it is not needed, and your doctor's recommendation is not likely to suffice in and of itself.

There are some things I have found that can help. The fastest seems to be a well-placed front-page article in the paper about how the state is not fulfilling its part of the contract. This can be a powerful tool, and the paper's legislative reporter is the one to call. On three different occasions, I have had to resort to asking a reporter to write one, and on all three occasions the request, which had been stalled in the appeals process, was mysteriously approved within a week of the article. Other times, the only intervention that worked seemed to be prayer.

The larger Shane grew, the more difficult it became for me to contain him. After a couple of years at our house, he was still having uncontrollable rages, sometimes several times a day. Although he was always sorry when he came to for the damage he had done, we just could not find a combination of medications that would give him any real relief at all. On top of that, each time a medication change was made he had to be hospitalized because he was completely uncontrollable while one drug was being decreased and before the next one approached a therapeutic level.

Still, we continued the process of trying to find just the right combination of medication and therapeutic intervention. In the meantime, Shane had been in and out of treatment centers and hospitals for years, while I fought with the state trying to get Adoption Assistance to make good on the contract guaranteeing his needs would be provided for. It was a futile and frustrating fight.

By the time Shane was thirteen, his strength finally reached the point that his doctors believed that it was no longer safe for him to be at home. Although he did not qualify for hospitalization because his problems were chronic rather than acute, he was so severely disturbed that he was incapable of functioning at school or in day care. No matter how I tried, I was unable to get the approval in writing, which the contract demanded before he could be sent to the wilderness treatment program his doctors recommended. For two and a half months, I lowered my workload to almost nothing so that I could stay home with him, while his doctors and I fought to get the state to approve the program. For two and a half months, I appealed from one level to the next as the request was turned down. For two and a half months, our meager income became more and more destitute, until finally my house went into foreclosure and I had to declare bankruptcy. Still, we fought with the state to get the approval we needed.

At the same time, my friend Carol was dying after a long battle with cancer. Many friends of hers came in from out of town towards the end to say goodbye, and some of them, including me, took turns caring for her. Finally, the call came a few hours after I had last been there. I was at work. Carol had died, and her husband would not let anyone into the house. Her friends were gathering on the porch, and he was asking for me. I was the only one he would let come in.

All I could do was look into the face of my next counseling client and say, "A friend of mine just died. I have to go." And I went.

After we lovingly cleaned the body and straightened up the house, I was able to convince Carol's husband to let in the friends who had continued in the meantime to gather on the porch. So in they came, in handfuls and singly, until the house was full. A police officer came, and asked if we had touched the body. "Only to take out all the needles and give her a bath and clean pajamas," we said. I thought the officer would arrest us on the spot, so sure she was that we had killed Carol and then destroyed the evidence. Finally, one of our friends was able to convince her that we weren't likely murder suspects, that hospice had been involved, and that her death was expected rather than premeditated.

Friends continued to gather. We made Carol a toe tag, since she had decided to donate her body to Meharry Medical College, and we began to sing and pray. "Free at last, Free at last, Thank God Almighty, She's Free at last." Then my friend Mauni asked about Shane, and I gave them the latest update. The approval still had not come.

"Maybe Carol could intervene on Shane's behalf," Mauni said. "Maybe Carol could be Shane's guardian angel, his patron saint." We laughed, oh, that it could be so, but still I asked aloud, "If there is anything you can do to help him, Carol, would you please do it *now?*"

As the evening went on, someone came down from the apartment upstairs and said I had a phone call. To this day, I have no idea how the caller found me there at that time, but it was someone I had worked for on a contract for the state years before. She wanted to know about all the trouble I was making on Shane's behalf. I started to explain, and asked how she knew about it. "All those people you've been bothering," she explained, "work for me." It turned out the appeal had continued to go up the ladder until it reached her office, even though I had no idea of her current position, or the fact that it was going up level by level until it got to her. "We were having a meeting, just now," she told me, "about Shane." She was calling to let me know that she had decided to approve the request for the wilderness program he so desperately needed.

Thank you, Saint Carol, for whatever you did on Shane's behalf. The program helped change his life.

⋯⋯

Consider...

What "guardian angels" do you know who might be willing to help with your child/ren? Are there those who might offer an outing once a week or once a month? How about someone who might commit to pray regularly for your child's healing and well being? What "patron saints" do *you* need? What would it take for you to ask?

An excellent attorney may be one kind of "guardian angel" you need but haven't yet considered. If you can afford one, have an attorney go over your adoption subsidy contract *before* you sign it. Have that attorney check to see if there is any way to provide for the eventuality that your child will need immediate care while the required authorization is being waited for. Have them check to see if there is some way to protect your interests. If you cannot afford a private attorney, check with the local legal services office or the legal clinic of a nearby law school.

NOTES

21. Flexibility

Along Came a Spider...

Family additions are like any change. No matter how exciting, no matter how good change is, it creates chaos. That is the reason that the Chinese character for chaos is formed by the combination of the characters for danger and opportunity. Change upsets the balance of things, and adding a new family member will upset everyone's balance for a while until the new order of things is determined. Add a new horse to a pasture, and the horses will jockey for position until the new horse's place in the herd is set. Get a new dog, and the old dogs will all start growling over their food until all of them have agreed on which one is the new leader of the pack. Add a new child, and everyone in the family starts stressing out until the new arrangements are familiar.

*This can be particularly excruciating for younger children if the new child that comes is out of the natural birth order. Add a baby or a younger child, and the older ones still feel secure in their positions, which are already determined. Only the youngest gets displaced, and in this case, it is to graduate upwards. Add an older child, however, and the chaos gets more dramatic. Suddenly, there is a new member of the family who has privileges and responsibilities that the younger ones have not yet earned. "Why does **he** get to stay up later than I do?" "Why does **she** get to date and I can't?" "You never let **us** watch R rated movies!"*

Another thing that may change with family additions is rules. For the first fifteen years and five children I parented, for instance, we got by on only one rule, "No one gets hurt." It was used to examine every activity from "You can't hit your brother, it hurts him," to, "It will hurt you later in life if you don't get finish your schoolwork now." When Shane came along, we had to add one more: "Follow directions the first time asked without comment." It did not preclude the possibility of arguing, but required that the argument follow compliance rather than precede it. With Brock's arrival, we had to add about thirty more.

Children are understandably concerned about the effect a new family member will have on them. They will undoubtedly get less of your individual attention. They may well receive a smaller portion of the family's financial resources. They will have to share everything in the household with yet one more person. And, if you are a part of a couple, that is true for your partner as well. Reassurance is in order, but only time will sort it out.

••

One day while Shane was at the wilderness program, something interesting happened at work. I got to the office to find a note in my mailbox that read, "Please see Jan or Donna ASAP." I wandered towards the back of the building thinking maybe it was office gossip, with absolutely no idea that the very short note would change my life.

"You know those two little boys?" she asked. Of course I did. Everyone in the office knew about Brock and Jacob, the two little boys we had placed for adoption more than once but proceeded to disrupt every placement we found for them. "They just disrupted again. They can stay where they are tonight, but we have to find a new placement for them by tomorrow and we don't have one lined up yet. Could you just take them home for the weekend?"

I knew better than to believe the "just for the weekend" part – I'd been in social work way too long to fall for that. But I was willing to take them home until another placement could be found, so the next day I met Brock, who got there first. He was indeed a handful, much smaller than his younger brother. His first words to me were, "I'm eight, but I'm almost nine, and I *know* how to get kicked out of a home." At least he thought he did. The battle was on.

The boys were still with me when I went for my next visit with Shane, even though no decisions had been made yet about what was to become of them. I was greatly concerned about how Shane would take the fact that while he was away from home in a wilderness program, there were two other little boys who were staying at his house. I took great pains to explain that they were just staying for a little while, and no one knew what would happen. I had no idea what his reaction would be, and did not want to do anything to make him feel threatened, because at that point, Noel was in college and my primary commitment was to Shane. The last thing I wanted was for someone else to come along, sit down beside me, and frighten Shane away.

Before I knew it, another youth in the program asked who the two little boys were who were playing outside the window.

"They are my two new little brothers," was Shane's reply.

....

Consider…

Children are frequently more adaptable than their parents. If you already have children at home, start by discussing with them your thoughts about adding more. Sometimes they can be very exact about what they want; other times, they can be definite about what they are not ready to face.

If you have a child already in counseling or psychotherapy, talk to that child's therapist about the child's readiness for a family addition.

Discuss with your agency worker the effect that new family members may have on children already in the family. Depending on the age of the child/ren you are considering and their handicaps (if any), talk about delayed reactions you and your child/ren are likely to face in years to come.

Every family has rules, even though they are frequently unspoken. What rules do you go by in your family? Put the cap back on the toothpaste? If you make a mess, clean it up? Make a list of your family rules. If and when a new child comes, talk about your rules and then post them on the refrigerator door so that there is no question about your expectations.

How can you imagine these rules changing to accommodate certain children and behaviors? Prepare yourself to be flexible and negotiate fairly.

❧ NOTES ☙

22. Gratification

Breakthrough

*When I was a counselor, our clinical consultant used to regularly admonish us to keep our goals small. This is also a helpful coping mechanism when parenting special-needs children. Having low enough expectations can provide you with multiple small victories to keep you going for a long time, while the hoped-for gratification of larger successes is delayed. (During one **particularly** difficult stage with the boys, my goals became so miniscule that in response to the question, "How are you?" I would regularly find myself answering, "EVERY day I don't kill them and they don't kill me is a GOOD day.") Big accomplishments can be years in the works – even ones that would take significantly less time with other children – but they are **absolutely** worth working towards and waiting for.*

▪▪

The wilderness program that Shane went to used peer pressure to effect change in teenagers' behavior by forcing them to conform to group expectations. No one did anything until everyone else did. That meant no one ate until everyone got to the new campsite and helped cook dinner. No one slept until everyone helped set up the tents. No one moved on to the next activity until everyone in the huddle agreed that the last problem had been resolved by the group.

For Shane, who still struggled with the effort of putting his feelings into words, the constant huddles forced him to discuss problems he would otherwise have been unable or unwilling to confront. Doc used chess the same way. Shane loved to play, but if he started to erupt, Doc would calmly put the game away and say no game was more important than their relationship. As Doc coached Shane through playing the game, he was also coaching him through dealing with the problems and frustrations of his life.

The whole time Shane was away at the wilderness program, he was brought home for weekly therapy sessions with Doc and the rest of the family. The two therapies worked in tandem, breaking down Shane's defenses while teaching him new tools for resolving his many problems. Little by little, they chipped away at the overwhelming obstacles he faced.

Although Shane was mostly past the "Parking Lot Therapy" stage by that time, one Wednesday when the wilderness program staff member brought him to Doc's office, he was terrible. He did *not* want to go into the office and talk to Doc, and the staff member who brought him that day was, well, less than helpful. The session was, for all appearance's sake, a disaster. The next week, it just so happened that Doc was going to be out of the office on Wednesday, the day of their weekly sessions, and there was no appointment scheduled. I knew it, the staff from the wilderness program knew it, and Doc knew it. Apparently, Shane did not.

The single most significant breakthrough in Shane's treatment happened the following week, just at a time when no one expected it. By the time he got to Doc's office, Shane was overwhelmingly distressed. Finally, after much work on Doc's part, he was able to discern that the reason Shane was so upset was that he had wanted to see Doc the week before, and Doc had let him down by not being there for him.

We were all astonished. There was certainly no way anyone could have guessed from Shane's behavior that he had wanted to see Doc – ever! Only two weeks before, it had been all we could do to physically get him into the office. Doc tried to explain to Shane that there had been no appointment scheduled the week before, but Shane wouldn't believe it. Finally, Doc pointed out that obviously everyone else knew, because no one had brought Shane to Nashville for the appointment. That was something even Shane couldn't argue with.

Then Doc started trying to explain that he had not known that it was important to Shane to see him. During the session two weeks previous, Shane had completely stonewalled him, refusing to hear or respond to anything he said. Doc said he was sorry, but he just didn't know it mattered to Shane. From Shane's behavior, he couldn't tell. And then the breakthrough came: Shane was able to put into words that yes, Doc was important to him. Shane wanted to know when he would see Doc again. He wanted to be able to count on it.

That very day, they began the ritual of the cards. At the end of that session, and at the end of every session since, Shane has demanded an appointment card with the time and day of their next appointment. Doc always writes something funny on it instead of Shane's name, which Shane almost always has to have someone else read to him. He never surrenders the cards to me, so sometimes I don't even know when the next appointment is, and sometimes he has collected twenty or thirty at a time.

He keeps them, he says, just in case he needs them. And he has counted on Doc to be there for him ever since.

▪▪

Consider…

As we get older, our perspective about time changes. Birthdays that used to be unbearably far apart come closer and closer together, until eventually they seem to be almost right on top of each other. The future once so far away has already past. This change in perspective makes it easier for us as adults to delay gratification than for our children. We may not *like* waiting for things, but at least we are better at it than they are. When you look towards the future, what rewards do you hope parenting will bring?

In the long run, what breakthroughs are you hoping to make with the child/ren you want to parent?

How long are you willing to wait?

Expect it to take at least ten times that long.

NOTES

23. STABILITY

You Just Don't Get Another Mother

Stability is something foster/adopted children typically do not have much experience with. Change, they know. Disappointment, they come to expect. Loss, they eat and breathe. But stability? That can be pretty scary. The longer a relationship goes on, the more they fear it will come to an end. It will probably be years before your children really believe that you will be there for them tomorrow, and the next day, and the next.

You are fighting against a legacy of caregivers who have let them down, abused them, taken them for granted, and dropped them like hot potatoes when they got tired of them. Expect to remind your child daily that you have already chosen them, that you choose them still today, and that you will continue to choose them tomorrow. Tell your child/ren over and over again that you have committed yourself to them for as long as they need you – even if you feel like giving up. It won't hurt you any to hear yourself say it, too.

At the end of nine months, Shane came home from the wilderness program more stable than he had ever been at any point up till then. He had been so much younger and more limited in his abilities than the rest of the boys that the group had more or less taken him on as their mascot. His current medications, although they had not been changed, had been in his system long enough that he was starting to get some relief, and the 24-hour-a-day peer pressure of the group had worked better than anything we had been able to do at home to help him learn to control his behavior.

Although Shane had feared when he left that he would never be able to come home, while we were preparing him to go and for his entire stay we repeated the family mantra: "You can go to treatment, or you can go to jail; but when you get out, you come back here, because you don't ever get another mother." Over and over I had repeated it for him, and when he had passes we would go to Doc's office, and we would say it there, too.

In the meantime, Brock and Jacob were still with me. No decision had been made yet about their long-term care. They had gone with us to family therapy each time Shane had a pass, and the adoption staff where I worked continued to try to find them a permanent placement.

Finally, one day Brock asked me if I would adopt him. I was quite taken by surprise, and replied that I didn't think he wanted to be adopted. His reply was that he just didn't want to be adopted by someone he didn't like. Still, my primary commitment at that time was to Shane, and all I could say was that I would talk to Shane's doctors and to Jacob and Brock's adoption workers, and see. For the next several months, we were in negotiations.

Whether or not it would hurt Shane was my primary concern. Finally, the decision was made that I would adopt Brock, who was so disturbed that no one else was likely to adopt him, but would allow Jacob, who all their placements had wanted to keep, to be adopted by someone else. Within days, Jacob sadly spoke the words that changed my mind: "It's okay. I understand why you won't adopt me. You only adopt bad children, and I'm not bad like my brother."

No matter how cruelly Brock treated him, Jacob still just desperately wanted to be with his "only full blood relative," his brother. So, in the end, Shane gained two new little brothers, who replaced, in part, the twin brothers he had lost years before. He reveled in being the big brother, and it turned out to be one of the best things that ever happened for him. Because they were there, he took it upon himself to learn to behave better, so that he could in turn help them. Like so many of us, he was willing to do for the ones he loved what he would never have done just for himself.

• •

Consider...

Taking on additional children is a challenge none of us can hope to accomplish by ourselves. As the proverb says, "It takes a whole village to raise a child." In order for you to be faithful to your child/ren over the long haul, what will it take?

Abused women often leave abusive men not because of what the man has done to them, but in order to protect their children. What do you know you need to do for yourself that you have so far been unwilling to do? Eat more vegetables? Lose weight? Watch less television? Read more books?

What difference would it make in your life if you knew you were setting an example for a child?

How many times are you willing to reassure a child that you will not give up? It helps if you just keep reminding yourself that you only have to say, "No, I will not give you up," one more time than your child can act out, "I am afraid you will."

≈ NOTES ≪

24. School Phobia

Broken Arms

For many children, school is a humiliating and miserable experience; for those with special needs, it can be especially horrible. School phobia may be something your child/ren have experienced for years before coming to you. It may begin after the move to your home. Or it may be that it will only reveal itself only after the child/ren have been in one place for long enough that they have begun to feel safe. Especially if a child has not felt safe before, s/he may be reluctant to leave you to go into an unfriendly and unpredictable environment.

School phobia may be subtle, with children feeling only mildly sick to their stomachs on Monday mornings when it is time to go back to school after the weekend, or it may be dramatic, accompanied by panic attacks if the subject is even touched upon. It may be something that can be addressed with understanding and gentle encouragement, or it may require therapy and more drastic interventions.

Shane hated school. Every Monday, without fail, for every year so far, he had been "too sick" to go to school. He was sick to his stomach, or sick in the head, or maybe even his fingernails or toenails or hair hurt. That was how we started on the routine of going to Doc's every Monday morning at 7:00 A.M. Shane wouldn't get in the car to go to school, but he would get in the car to go to Doc's.

Each week when we left the appointment, I would drive to his school and just sit there in the parking lot, refusing to leave until he got out – no matter how long it took. He was so predictable that if he really did get sick on another day, not even his brothers would believe him. "You can't be sick," they'd say. "It's not Monday."

Some time after Jacob and Brock had come, Shane decided he had been made fun of for being sick for the last time. Arms curled tightly across his chest in Doc's waiting room one Monday morning at 7:00 A.M., "I can't go to school," he insisted.

"Why not, Shane," his brothers cynically asked, "are you sick?"

"No," he replied in all seriousness. "My arms are broken."

Consider…

What was your school experience like? Did you like it? Hate it? Look forward to going? Dread it?

Talk to your child and to his or her teachers. What do the teachers think about your child's acclimation to school? What is your child's experience? What does your child think would make it better?

If your child seems to be in great distress, make an appointment to meet with the entire teaching team. What is contributing to the distress? Bullies? Work that is too hard? Too much? Being made fun of by other children? How can these things be addressed?

Does your child's therapist or medical doctor need to be involved?

NOTES

25. Vacations

Buddha, the Boy

Just as it is hard to determine reasonable expectations for unusual children, it is hard to decide on reasonable vacations for the families of which they are a part. While every child may want to go to the beach, or the amusement park, or the mountains, it may not be wise or prudent to take your particular child there. If you do make the decision to take your child/ren to certain locations, it may be necessary to make special accommodations for any special needs.

Small children prone to getting lost can be taken to places where there are large crowds if they are connected to their parents by an arm's length rope connecting their belt to their parents'. (You have no idea how much easier this is than holding hands until you have tried it. You will want to make sure the rope or leash is not so long that either of you gets tangled in it. Fasten it securely at the back of your child's belt, and at the side of yours. Kids will not be able to quickly undo it themselves, and will appreciate having both their hands free. So will you.) Older children can be dressed in matching t-shirts with clearly identifiable logos so they can be spotted easily in a crowd or described to the park staff. (The ones my boys wore were in bright colors with tigers on them underneath which was the saying, "Born to be Wild." Truer words were hard to find.) Children who cannot swim can be outfitted in body suits that have the life jackets built in. (Some of the ones they have these days even have the zippers up the back so that small children cannot escape from their life jackets without your assistance.) Children who are unable to tolerate long trips away from home can be taken on multiple short trips within a day's drive of home. Children who are incontinent can sleep on waterproof sheets taken with you to a motel. Almost anything is possible if you just plan far enough ahead.

Occasionally, as a mother, I find myself agreeing to do something and afterwards have no idea what possessed me to do so. Driving the boys to visit Noel in Missoula, Montana was one of those. We lived in Nashville, Tennessee at the time – way too far for any one person in their right mind to think it is a good and reasonable idea to drive with a car full of boys! But one summer, we did it anyway.

Shane, Brock, Jacob, and one of Noel's high school friends all joined me one evening in my seven-passenger van: five folks and WAY too much stuff, crammed into every conceivable space. My goal was to spend no more days in the car than necessary. While the boys slept I would occasionally stop to nap, but as much as possible, I drove all night. I used to call it, "Making Your Sleep Disorder Work For You." As we passed landmarks, I would wake the boys up. "Wake up, guys!" for instance, "It's the Saint Louis Arch." That sort of thing.

By the time we arrived in Missoula, where Noel was an RA for his dorm, the kids were climbing the walls from being cooped up in the car so long – exactly what Noel, whose job was to keep folks quiet during exams, did not need. His little brothers were creating havoc in his room. After a couple of days of chaos the semester ended, and Noel and his roommate climbed into the van with the rest of us (now up to seven people, one in each seat, plus even more stuff, plus camping equipment we added in Missoula) and we set off for Glacier National Park.

Somewhere along the way, Shane decided he had endured enough. When we stopped for gas, he took his blanket and stormed off, tromping down the highway until he finally stopped, spread out his blanket under a tree, collapsed upon it, and refused to budge. All the rest of us could do was wait. We couldn't do a thing to convince him to get back into the van with us. Finally, ever so slowly, he began to calm down. Eventually, he sat up, struck a meditating pose, and began to hum. For the first time in his life, he was finally able to laugh at himself, and even had us take his picture: Buddha, meditating under the tree. Only when he was ready did he climb back into the car, and we were able to take off again.

We spent a couple of days at Glacier, during which time Shane gloried in being one of the "big boys" for the very first time. He went hiking and swimming with them, while I camped out with Brock and Jacob. Shane even joined the college guys in jumping off a bridge – one of those events I was really glad I didn't know about until after it was over. They all claimed it was safe, but if I had known, I'd have been terrified. All I could imagine in my mother's mind were all sorts of dangerous rocks under the surface of the water below the forty-foot drop from the bridge.

From Glacier we went back to Missoula, where we dropped off Noel and his roommate, and headed south. For a little while, Neal's friend drove while I napped. When I woke up the gas tank was into reserve, and there was no exit in sight. The boys said a sign a while back had read "Gas Station, 10 miles," but when we got to the exit there was no gas station anywhere to be found – only prairie for as far as we could see. The dilemma resulted in what became for years Shane's favorite joke: "The sign must have been wrong," he said. "It said GAS station, but they must have meant GRASS station." We could hardly believe Shane made a joke, especially a play on words, and laughed till we thought we would fall out of the car.

Down we continued to travel until we reached the Grand Canyon (for those of you who are imagining this on the map, you will know that the Grand Canyon is REALLY out of the way, but the boys wanted to see it). Big mistake. Can you imagine one mother with only two arms trying to hold on to one young man who was afraid of heights and two boys with severe ADHD, while trying to keep the three of them from falling off the edge of the cliff that was the Grand Canyon? It was not a pretty picture, to say nothing of the fact that after all the days of driving, they were bored within fifteen minutes. ("All it does is just sit there," they complained. "It doesn't DO anything.") And then they were ready to go.

Back into the car, we headed across the desert, where more jokes were made about Mexican Running Dogs than you can imagine, and more verses were sung to "I've Got the Blues" than you could bear, and on we drove to Lubbock, Texas. We ate breakfast with my little sister, whom the boys had not yet met, and then back towards Nashville on I-40, sweet I-40, all the way home. We have not, and will not, ever do it again, but it was a glorious vacation. It was a great thing to do. Once.

Consider...

Before you start planning, check the provisions in your foster/adoption contract about taking your child out of state. Some contracts require worker permission to take a child in state custody across the state line, even for a short vacation.

What were your favorite vacations when you were a kid? What would be your idea of a good time now? Where do your child/ren want to go? Do the answers have anything in common? If not, is there anywhere you can go where things are at least close in proximity?

Choose a vacation that is sensible, affordable, and offers something for everyone, every day if possible. It is better to do something reasonably priced even if it is smaller and closer to home than to attempt something too big and too far away and then to be so broke that you are constantly worried and no one is having fun.

Each person does not have to like *everything* you do, as long as there is some fun for *everyone* at regular intervals. If you need to, remind the child/ren as you go along, "We're doing this because your brother wants to. Tonight, we're doing what you want to. Tomorrow we're going to do what your mom wants to." It will help them wait more patiently if they know everyone is taking turns and that it is not necessarily true that EVERYONE is having fun except them.

NOTES

26. Naming

And the Winner Is…

When older children are placed for adoption, parents are faced with an issue that never comes up with infants, and rarely arises with foster kids, who generally keep their names: older children want some input into their adoptive names. Quite possibly, your child/ren will want to continue being called by names you can't stand. They may want to hold on to a family name because it is all they have left of their family, while you may want to give them your own name or a family name. Choices may require delicate negotiation if your child is old enough to know what is going on.

Giving a child complete control over what s/he is going to be called may not be the best of ideas, but neither is it fair to impose your will on a child who already identifies with a name s/he may have been going by for years. Other children, who may have been through multiple foster placements, may have already gone by a variety of names before they came to you. A child may have extremely strong feelings about the issue, or few at all.

No matter what the child's position is, it is helpful if a decision is agreed upon before the adoption is finalized. While names can, of course, be legally changed after that time, it certainly is more difficult and expensive than it is during the adoption process. Talk to your child/ren about the issue ahead of time. Try, if possible, to lead them to negotiate a settlement that everyone can feel good about.

This story must be prefaced with the notation that my memory of how this happened is not at all the same as Noel's memory of the same events. The two versions are, in fact, so different that they remind me of one day when a husband I knew finally exploded with how much he hated his wife's terrible spinach soufflé, which she made, according to him, all the time. The wife was totally confused, and told her husband that she only made it because she thought he liked it. It turned out that twenty or so years before, when she was trying out new recipes after they first married, she fixed this dish. She said she *didn't* like it, but he, trying to be nice, praised it and told her how much he *did* like it. She, believing he was telling the truth, had continued to fix it for him – frequently – for all the years since. It turned out he had hated it, and was, as she was, just trying to be nice. Noel's and my memories of this story are a little like that. Each of us, it turns out, was just trying to be nice.

My recollection is that as the court date for Brock and Jacob's adoption approached, my one birth son, Noel, stated to me that he was having difficulty with the fact that there would now be three children who shared my last name, and he was going to be the only one to have a different last name than the rest of us. He had been named for his great-grandfather and we had called him by my grandfather's name when he was born, but at the age of three he had made the decision to go by his middle name, Noel, which was my maiden name. I had started using that surname again after his dad and I divorced. Noel had his father's surname for his last name.

When Shane was the only one who shared my last name it did not seem to bother Noel, but with Jacob and Brock's adoption, I was suddenly going to have three other sons with a different last name than his. He talked more and more about the fact that he could not have the same last name as the rest of us, because that would make his name, "Noel Noel."

We began tossing around the idea of all of us, as a family, choosing a new last name, and after a couple of months of discussion, that is what we did. In the end, we decided upon my mother's maiden name. It was already part of Noel's name because he had been named for his maternal great-grandfather.

I gave each of the boys the option of choosing his own first name, but that turned out not to have been one of my better ideas. Brock and Jacob loved a series of movies about three little boys who were ninjas, and chose as their new names "Rocky" and "Tum-Tum" respectively. Shane, for his part, chose "Steven Segal" (his favorite movie star) as his new name. No amount of subtle negotiation would budge any of them. In the end, I exercised my veto power as the mother and told them that they simply could not choose anyone else's name. They had to choose a name that would be only theirs, and I would give them family names for their middle names.

Given the new limits, Kenneth Brock decided he would choose as his first name Brock, which he had gone by for years even though it was actually his middle name, and Jacob decided he would just stay Jacob. Brock was given my Uncle Ben's name for a middle name since my Aunt Kathie and Uncle Benny had never had children of their own; Jacob was given the middle name Edward for his half-sister's grandfather, since Patricia's grandparents had grandparented him almost all of his life.

Shane, for his part, decided he wanted to legally change his name, too, even though his adoption was already final. He chose as his new first name the nickname he was most often called at school, even though he still continued to answer to Shane. His middle name became Murray, for my brother and another of my uncles. And in spite of complaints from all three of the younger boys that every time they wrote their names for the entire rest of their lives, they would have to write two more letters ("Did I have *any* idea how many letters that would add up to over their lifetimes?") each and every one of us legally changed our surname to the same thing.

••

Consider…

If your child/ren are old enough at the time of placement to care about the name they are to be given or called, talk to them about name possibilities and preferences.

Try to set parameters that would make it possible for your child/ren to participate in the choice. You have to be willing to give up naming someone after your favorite old uncle Eldridge, if your child can't stand that name. The child is the one who has to live with the choice the rest of his or her life, not you. Giving more than one choice that is palatable is helpful, as in "Would you rather be called _____ or _____?"

Be prepared to live with a name you dislike, if it is significantly important enough to your child. To you, it is a name. To your child, it is who they are.

NOTES

27. GOALS

Finger Lickin' Chicken

When our children have any one or more of a multitude of handicapping conditions, it is frequently difficult to decide what reasonable expectations for them might be. This includes reasonable expectations for behavior and success, as well as for future goals. Because these children have probably already been faced with a multitude of failures, it is important to set reasonable, attainable goals for them. Multiple small goals can make palatable the large goal they lead to. Short-term goals can be anything from "I expect you to make your bed before you go outside to play," to, "I am going to help you learn one multiplication fact before supper." Longer-term goals can include such things as, "I believe that you can graduate from high school, and I am not going to let you drop out," or, "I know you can learn to cook fried chicken if you just practice long enough…"

One of the young people who rotated in and out of our home was Rozita. Rozita came to live with us when she aged out of the foster care system and had nowhere to go. She is one of the most interesting people you can imagine, and Shane is completely devoted to her.

Among her other many talents, Rozita is a superb cook. Her fried chicken is, as they say, to die for, and Shane was determined to learn how to make it. Patiently, she would show him how to do it, time after time, and eventually he got to be wonderful at it. I cannot begin to compete with his competence in this department, and he is rightfully proud of himself for his skill.

No other way than Rozita's will do, and he delights in making fun of my efforts and telling me what I have done wrong. I am in no position to argue with him, because his version of her chicken is much better than what I make myself. Ever since learning how to do it, Shane has had it in his mind that he would like to open a restaurant. If he would just learn to cook a few more things with the same enthusiasm he has for frying his finger lickin' chicken, he could.

Consider…

What skills and interests do your child/ren exhibit? What would be reasonable ways to encourage them to develop these abilities?

What long-term goals do you have for your child/ren that they may not be able to accept or take on for themselves? What goals do they have for themselves that you are unwilling to accept for them?

Talk to your child's therapist about reasonable short-term and long-term goals. Invite your child to join the discussion and participate in making a list of goals to work toward. Let your child help choose small rewards to earn for milestones along the way.

NOTES

28. Change

Chef Campbell

For many special-needs children, change has been dangerous. They have been moved around a lot, people are frequently scary, and the security of a familiar environment is something they want to hold on to at all costs. That makes school an interesting challenge. Maybe your child has become attached to a certain teacher or aide and that person is no longer available. Maybe s/he has become so entrenched into a certain routine that when the routine has to be changed for one reason or another, chaos follows. Maybe s/he has learned how to be successful in a self-contained classroom but then graduates to a grade where that is no longer a possibility.

Special-needs kids frequently need to be encouraged to stretch beyond their comfort level, but the bottom line is that every child has a right to an educational environment in which s/he can be successful. If your child is having a hard time in his or her regular classroom, ask your school for a copy of the list of rights of special education children. If, after reading it, it sounds like your child needs that kind of support, start advocating for it. In some cases the school may have begun the process before you ask, but in other cases it takes years before that happens.

One Asperger's child I know was certified for special education only after telling her new therapist that she'd had a really good day at school that day, saying she had "only cried one time all day." Shocked, the therapist asked how many times she usually cried at school, and Rachael replied, "At least three times." For years, the child's teachers had ignored her distress. The therapist heard it differently, and with her persistent intervention Rachael was soon certified for the services she needed. No child should ever have to be that miserable that long.

As the parent of a special-needs child, you have the right to attend the school team meetings, and if your child is certified to be in need of special education services, you have the right to legal representation at the meetings if you need it. Being pushed beyond our comfort level is one way we all grow, and it is one way our children grow, too. But the encouragement needs to be done gently, and it also needs to be done appropriately.

When Shane finally got to high school, he was confronted with a dilemma. Up until that point, he had always been in what was termed a "self-contained classroom." The classroom was designed for children who were fragile in one way or another, and as much as he hated school, it was a somewhat safe environment for him to be in. Even at that, change was so difficult for him that each time he changed schools he ended up repeating his first year at the new school because he would lose a year's instructional time just trying to get used to the new environment. We got permission for him to attend the high school that was only a block down the street from his junior high so that he could still go to the home of his surrogate grandparents, Granny and Pop Webb, every day after school – but there were still a lot of changes to face.

High school was a whole new ball game. While it was possible for him to get his academic classes in the self-contained classroom (a portable building separate from the rest of the school), electives required for graduation had to be taken in the high school building among the greater high school population. Shane did not deal well with change, people, or chaos, and the high school building meant all those things. It was going to be a challenge.

Finally, he agreed that he would like to take Chef Campbell's cooking classes as electives. He loved to cook, and that love might make going into the building worthwhile. To get into Chef's class, students were required to write an essay about why they wanted to take the class. From these essays, she chose the class members. Shane dictated his to me, and I typed it on the computer for him. Everyone who read his essay loved it.

He started out by saying he needed to be in the class because food was very important to him. He talked about the fact that being a good cook was one way to get girls to like you. He talked about knowing people who were diabetic and how it was important to know what you could cook that would not kill them. He talked about Jacob's kidney disease, and how he wanted to know how to cook whatever his brother could eat. And he ended by saying that anyone who looked at him (he was by that time quite well nourished) could tell that food was very important to him. Even Chef loved the essay. He got in *and* he convinced himself that taking the class was worth the risk.

••

Consider…

Think about times when you have been forced into change. Maybe it was in school, or at work. Would you have done it if you didn't have to? What would you have wanted to be different? What helped you get through it?

Now think about how much more difficult that change would have been if you had physical or mental limitations. Think about the type of child you would like to adopt. What could you do to help that child?

How can you deal with your own feelings of frustration and powerlessness to make life easier for the one you love?

NOTES

29. Laughter

Horse Sense

*The ability to laugh at oneself is hard to develop, but well worth the effort. If we can learn to take ourselves a little less seriously, we often find that life itself is easier to take. That is true for our children, too. Who hasn't been laughed at by someone who said, "We're not laughing AT you, we're laughing WITH you," even though the recipient of the laughter knew better? But what if we **could** laugh at ourselves, too? By taking our own selves less seriously, we as parents may set an example that helps our children roll with the punches instead of being overwhelmed by them.*

One year on the fourth of July, Shane bravely took off to the cabin at the lake with Brock, Jacob, and their half-sister's family. Patricia's dad, Brian, still tells the story of sitting on the shore with Shane while Jacob and Patricia lit fireworks on the dock. Shane wasn't having any part of it. Finally, Jacob lit a mortar on the dock without placing it in a tube or even pointing it towards the sky, and it blew up right under Jacob and Patricia's feet. Brian and Shane exploded into giggles and belly laughter after Shane, who was always sensitive about not being able to do everything that everyone else could do, blurted out, "Even *I* have more sense than to do THAT!"

Consider...

What wounds do you carry from being laughed at by others? Looking back at the same events now, does the change in perspective give you any insight into what it was that the laughers thought funny at the time?

How can you model for your child/ren a healthy perspective on your own finitude? How can you be realistic about your humanity and limitations without being self-deprecating? What possibilities really *could* open up for your family if you didn't think you had to appear to be perfect?

ಐ NOTES ಐ

30. Medical Care

The Bad Patient

Medical issues are rarely fun to deal with, even for folks who are otherwise "normal." For special-needs children, it gets even more complicated. If the child's special needs are mental, there may be difficulty in comprehending upcoming procedures, resulting in an even higher level of fear and lower level of cooperation than in most other people. If the child's special needs are physical, you and your child may be in and out of hospitals and doctor's offices more than you ever thought possible. For many children, the difficulty is a combination of both mental and physical issues.

Good planning can often help smooth the way. Not only can your child's mental health provider give you suggestions about things that can be helpful in dealing with your child, s/he can also call or write letters to the child's medical care health provider in order to give that person suggestions on creative ways of dealing with the patient. Sometimes, scheduling can be important – does the child do better at certain times of day, and if so, can the physician accommodate that need? Sometimes medication is an important issue – does the child need to take certain medications on the day of the procedure or examination? How can anxiety be reduced? Can a trial trip be made to the facility just so the child gets familiar with the lay of the land? Is it possible for the child to meet personnel ahead of time?

Sometimes, it is helpful to think through what WE would like if we weren't embarrassed to ask, and then to advocate for it for our children. We might never ask for anti-anxiety medication for ourselves, for instance, but requesting it for our children may make a lot of sense. We might suffer through being cold without asking for that extra blanket, but most hospitals even have heated blankets if you or your child needs one. We might let someone treat us without asking questions, but our children might need every question asked and answered. Before you let hospital personnel subject your child to an invasive procedure, ask if it is really necessary – sometimes it is not, and is instead an elective procedure that you can refuse. And if you are in a hospital and are having difficulty getting your question answered, the magic words are, "I'd like to speak to the Attending." The Attending will be doctor who can answer almost anything for you, or get the answer if it is not already known. If by any chance the Attending is not available, ask for a Chaplain. Chaplains can do more than just address religious needs. They can help walk you through the system and find the answers to your questions. They can find the Attending for you, too.

• •

Shane is a terrible patient. He frequently doesn't understand what is going on, which makes medical procedures frightening for him, and being in pain almost always triggers his PTSD. He is terrified of being abandoned, so when he is afraid and/or in pain, he always wants someone else there with him, and when his anxiety is high, he talks to them nonstop. It is enough to drive you crazy.

For me, the most vivid example of this will always be the night he had some intestinal bug. He was already in high school at the time, big enough, you would think, to take care of himself, and I had already gotten up with him about a half dozen times during the night.

I was exhausted and still had to go to work the next morning. Finally, I heard him in the bathroom downstairs again, and felt I just could not possibly get up one more time. Surely, I thought, he could throw up by himself. I was wrong.

After a few minutes, I heard him downstairs beating on the bathroom walls, and yelling. *"If I"* THUMP *"can't sleep"* THUMP *"nobody's"* THUMP *"gonna sleep!"* THUMP. You just can't argue with logic like that.

■ ■

Consider…

Imagine being sick and confused and too young to understand what is going on. What do you think would make you feel better if you had no words to help you? Would another's presence be enough?

When you are sick now, in either mental or physical distress, what are the things most likely to make you feel better? Are they the same things that worked when you were five, or seven, or twelve, or in your teens?

What keeps you from asking for the things you need to make yourself feel better? Would it be any easier if you were asking for someone else?

When you are physically exhausted and need a break from care giving, what are some ways to get one and also make sure your child is still attended to?

NOTES

31. SURRENDER

Shane and Earline Throw a Party

*Everyone has received one gift or another that wasn't wanted. Usually we smile, act pleased, and either put the gift in a drawer or on a shelf, or we return it to the store for a refund or exchange. But if the giver is one of our children, the interaction gets a little more complicated. We truly do **not** wish to hurt our children's feelings. We really **are** grateful that they have thought of us, and we want them to know that their gifts to us are important.*

So... in the case of our children, what do we do when we get a gift that is absolutely unwanted? The question of how to decline without causing harm is complicated. Add in the factor of a child with special needs who has already been rejected way too many times, and you've got an interesting dilemma on your hands. To refuse the gift is to refuse a part of the child, and sometimes they cannot be redirected, no matter how hard you try...

One of my old friends used so say, "You have to choose which trench you're willing to die in." Trust me. This is not the one.

••

It was the Friday before my birthday – my last birthday of the millennium – and Earline called me at the office. "I know how you feel about having people at your house," she said, "so I'm just calling to warn you." *Oh, no,* I thought. *What now?* It turned out Shane and Earline were planning a party.

To fully appreciate how much I hated having people come to my house, you'd have to understand what Brock was like in those years. At age twelve, he had pretty much quit punching holes in the walls, urinating on the furniture and breaking doors... as long as I didn't fix anything. A *tabula rasa* was just more of an invitation than he could turn down. After replacing six doors and fixing endless holes, I had pretty much given up, waiting until his behavior improved enough to warrant fixing things again, so I tried to avoid having company like the plague.

It would also be helpful for you to know that by Friday afternoon each week, I was usually exhausted. Juggling kids (with their constant struggles), schools (two, on different sides of town, requiring a daily commute of about an hour and fifteen minutes twice a day), doctor's appointments (usually for a total of five to six hours per week, on a week when everyone was doing well), work (which was actually my favorite part of the day, taking place only during the hours kids were at school, since Shane couldn't ride the bus, and Brock had been kicked out of every after school program in town), to say nothing of trying to keep the family in groceries and spending time at the drugstore waiting for prescriptions to be filled.

It was a very wearing schedule. By Friday afternoons, I just wanted to go home. On a *really* big Friday night out, we drove down the road a few blocks, rented four movies (one PG-13 rated movie of choice for each boy and one for me), popped microwave popcorn, and had a movie marathon. Maybe we'd even grab a burger.

On my birthday, you know, I had these fantasies. It would be quiet. The kids would be nice to me. I wouldn't have to listen to anyone yell all day. Then, as I said, Earline called. "Clean your house," she warned, "Because company's coming. Shane and I are throwing you a party."

"Oh, no, you're not," I replied, "or if you do, it is not happening here. If you're throwing me a party you'll have to find another place to have it." So they did.

I have never been much of one for parties. By far and large, for most of my life, I have avoided crowds like the plague. My Christmas shopping is always completed by Halloween, so that I can avoid stores and parking lots for the busy season. I hate going out to the malls at any time of year, and almost never do. I am just not a party person.

For years, I have indulged myself in exactly the same birthday ritual: lunch with my friend Martha, get the tree with the kids (whichever kids it happened to be that year), build a fire, put up the tree, decorate it, remember old friends. You can only imagine the joy with which I look forward to and participate in the annual event. I have no idea why this one year, much against my wishes, Shane and Earline decided to throw me a birthday party. No matter how much I did not want to participate, they were so excited about the idea I just couldn't bring myself to tell them no. I found myself being dragged into it, needless to say, as a reluctant participant.

"What would you like to eat?" they asked.

"Chocolate cake and vanilla ice cream," I answered. (Of course!)

"You can't have that. We've already planned the menu." (Then you asked me, *WHY?*)

"What do you want for a birthday present?"

"A Christmas ornament." (Always!)

"Well then, we'll have to have a ride to get our party supplies." (Oh, Great. Just what I want *least*.)

I may not have been kicking and screaming on the outside, but that was definitely how I felt inside as Shane and Earline let me know they needed a ride to the mall, of all places. Earline didn't drive, which meant they had no way to go anywhere unless I took them, and I never go there anytime I can avoid it – which is almost always. But at night on the tenth of December? AAUGH!

So there I was, sacrificing the Friday night on which I usually collapsed after work, to take Shane and Earline to the mall so they could get whatever they needed for the party that I didn't want anyway but was scheduled to take place the following day. The traffic was terrible, and the trip took hours. It was, of course, a weekend night in the middle of the Christmas shopping season, and the parking lot and the mall were packed. In desperation, I stayed in the car, literally weeping with exhaustion and totally overwhelmed by the number of people all around, while Shane and Earline shopped. It turned out that the first stop was for Christmas ornaments, my favorite birthday gift.

Most of my friends, knowing that was what I loved most to receive, had gotten into the habit of gifting me each year with birthday gifts of special and often symbolic ornaments. Each year as I put the ornaments on the tree, I would remember the giver and give thanks for my love for them and their love for me. I loved the ornaments, and I loved the ritual. But Shane and Earline stayed inside for what seemed forever, coming out at last with not just one ornament, but bags of ornaments; not one special one, but boxes and boxes of shiny balls.

By the time they got back out to the car, I had for the most part been able to stop crying. I got out and helped them get their bags into the car, thinking that at last I could go home and collapse. But no. "Now, we have to go to Old Time Pottery," they said.

"I only agreed to go to one place," I replied.

"We have to go," they insisted.

"Why?"

"We need hooks for the ornaments."

"I have hooks, we don't need to go."

"How many?"

"How many do you need?"

"Eighty-four."

"WHAT?" They bought eighty-four ornaments. I only wanted one.

Next, they wanted a ride to the grocery store. "We've got to stop by the grocery store on the way home. It'll only take a minute." I didn't know why I should bother. It wasn't as though *I* was getting to pick out what I wanted for my own birthday dinner, since they had already planned the menu. I couldn't even pick the flavor of the cake. Gritting my teeth, I begrudgingly took them to the grocery. An hour and fifteen minutes later they came out. I delivered Earline and the stuff to her apartment, and took Shane and the other boys home and put them to bed. The plan was for me to have Shane back at her place by 7:30 the next morning so that they could start cooking.

The next morning, the Saturday of my birthday, I couldn't sleep long enough to recover from the night before because I had to take Shane to Earline's. We got up early and headed to her place, but were surprised to discover when we got there that she wasn't home. It turned out she had gone swimming with a friend. Exhausted and frustrated, I took a disappointed Shane back home again.

Eventually, Earline called, wanting to know where Shane was, and if I would bring him back, which I did. More and more of the details drifted my way as I started getting phone calls. Among the other guests, they had invited my oldest foster daughter, Mary, to the party – which was to take place at Tommy and Lauren's house. The problem was that Mary didn't have a ride, either. Would I go and get her? To that one, I finally was able to put my foot down. No, I would not go get her. She lived over forty-five minutes away, and there was no way I was going to spend three precious hours of the little time left to me on my birthday making two round trips to her house.

Well, how about if I went and got _____? And Earline mentioned a name I didn't recognize at all. "Who is *that?*" I wanted to know. It turned out Earline had invited someone I didn't even know to the party, because it was an older friend of hers, "and you know how seniors love a party." Since she was already invited and only lived a few blocks from Earline, I couldn't figure out any way to get out of that one. Even though I did not know her, we went and got her, too.

In the end, the dinner that Shane and Earline cooked and took to Tommy and Lauren's was wonderful. We had fried chicken and macaroni and cheese, Shane's favorite foods. There was enough food for about forty people, even though only eight were there, and I survived the party. I do love Shane, and I do love Earline, and I *really* do appreciate their good intentions. But on the way home when they said, "We'll do better next year," all I could do was pray, "*Please, God, deliver me from the good intentions of those who love me.*" I hope I never, never, ever, have another birthday party again. Leave me to my boring ritual. One party is enough for any one lifetime.

• •

Consider...

Think back to a time you tried hard to be kind or to please someone only to have it fall flat. Maybe you spent a lot of time choosing a gift that was clearly a disappointment when it was opened, or maybe you went to give blood and were turned down. What was that like for you?

Think about a time when someone spoke unkindly about one of your parents or siblings. Did it feel as though the unkind words cut right through you? How about if someone said something wonderful about a member of your family? Did you bask in the glory, too?

Children have an even harder time distinguishing between themselves and the world around them than we do as adults. If we speak unkindly of a member of their family – birth, foster, *or* adopted – then by association we condemn them, too, even if that family member was cruel to them. If we refuse the child's offering of a gift – even if we don't want it – we reject both the child and the child's fragile love for us, too.

What are *you* willing to put up with for the sake of one you love?

NOTES

32. Reciprocity

Adult Day Care

Children, regardless of ability or disability, have the capacity not only to receive but also to give something back to the world around them. For the most severely handicapped, it may be that what they give most often to the world is the opportunity for others to serve, but even that can be an occasion of joy for the caregiver. For many children, it is the delight they demonstrate at even the most simple experiences that changes their parents' world for the better. Still others grow up to enter into caring professions themselves, becoming teachers, doctors, foster or adoptive parents, or aides.

Every child with the capacity to do so needs to learn that giving back to the world around us is as important as receiving. It gives us purpose and sets us apart from those who would use and abuse the helpless and needy. Giving back to the world in one way or another can help children feel good about themselves as well as prepare them for productive lives as adults.

Finding just the right venue for each child to learn this lesson – and to be successful at it – is tricky. As is true for everyone else in the world, special-needs children like doing one thing more than another. Some hard-to-place kids have the ability and willingness to do certain things but not others. Finding just the right balance can change lives.

■ ■

During the last three years of high school, Shane volunteered with an adult day care program almost every day after school and every day that school was out. He loved Lynn, who ran the program, and he loved helping the old people in the group.

Shane would get them coffee, trying determinedly to get each one exactly right (in a particular cup, two creamers, or extra sugar, however it was that the senior liked it). He would help them get up and move around, set the table and help feed them lunch, play games with them, call bingo for them. Whatever the participants wanted was his goal. As he gained confidence in helping them, Lynn told us that he was better at his job than most of the college students she had as interns. After Shane's first year as a volunteer there, the director of the agency told Lynn, Shane and myself that Lynn could hire him for one of their paying jobs as soon as he finished high school.

The motivation was amazing. For years he had hated school, but after he was promised a job, each morning that he was "too sick" to go to school, he would remind himself that he had to have a high school diploma. Nothing was more important to him than that diploma. He discovered that he wanted a diploma, because he wanted that job. Multiple times every day he would talk about it. He had to have a diploma, because he wanted that job. Not just any job. That job. He would talk about it when he got up in the morning getting ready for school. He would talk about it after school, how he made it through another day. He would talk about how he loved the adult day program when he got home at night, and about what each person in the program had done that day.

There was nothing he wanted more than to work for Lynn, and the diploma became the embodiment of how to get the job.

⋯⋯

Consider…

Giving something back to the world around them can change your child/ren's outlook on the world. What kinds of caring activities do they like to participate in? Do they like to baby-sit younger siblings? Help cook family meals? Take the dog for a walk? Read to someone who can't read for him or herself?

What opportunities are available in your community for children and teens to not only receive from the world around them but also to give back something to it? Would s/he rather be a candy-striper at the hospital than take out the trash? Would passing out lunches at a homeless program be more interesting than volunteering to help shelve books at the local library?

What sacrifices would it take on your part to make opportunities like these possible for your child? If you can't provide transportation yourself, for instance, could you find someone else who would? If your child is interested in something outside your comfort level, can you find another willing adult who might serve as a mentor?

Chances are that your children will not appreciate having been loved by you until later in their lives. While they are younger, they will more likely either fear it will not last or take for granted that you have taken them in. When they are teenagers, they may rebel against it. So what else can you do in your own life to demonstrate to them the importance of being productive, caring members of society?

✻ NOTES ✼

33. LOVE

43 Minutes, More or Less

Love is never easy. From the time children are in elementary school and find out that the schoolmate they have a crush on likes someone else, children's hearts are waiting to be broken. It only makes things worse if their families of origin have broken their hearts, too.

These children will attach too easily to anyone who gives them a second glance. They have no idea what appropriate boundaries are. They will not like the people you want them to. They will do stupid things for love – things you know better than, so why don't they? They will get into trouble for following their hearts instead of their heads. They will love when they should be cautious, and they will be cautious when the situation calls for loving with abandon. In short, your foster and adopted children will be just like you.

When Brian took Patricia, Brock, Jacob, and Shane to the local amusement park, they ran across someone Brian hadn't met before. She started following them around and talking to them, and riding with them on the rides. She was especially interested in Shane, and Brian assumed they were classmates.

The girl had ridden with them on several rides, talking to them in the lines, when Brian noticed her whispering in Shane's ear. The younger kids were all keeping a very close eye on them, and were actively acting as chaperones, as the group collectively noticed Shane and the girl dropping further and further behind them. The rest of the group kept stopping and turning around, watching and waiting for Shane and his friend to catch up, until finally one time they turned around to discover that the two teenagers were over in the bushes, kissing. The chaperones lept into action, but the kissing had already been done.

The little boys swear it was only ten to fifteen minutes, and Shane swears it was at least an hour, but Brian, who was the only one there with a watch, insists that it was 43 minutes from the time they met her until she and Shane were kissing. By that time, Brian thought she must have been Shane's girlfriend, and didn't think a whole lot about it until they got home. It wasn't till they got back to my house and I started asking questions, that we discovered the truth. Shane had never met the girl before in his life. Yet, he was kissing her in 43 minutes – or more – or less. Depending on who you ask. And depending on who you believe.

Consider…

What is an appropriate response to a child with a broken heart?

If it is appropriate to let your fourth grader stay home one day from school for a little extra attention the first time it happens, is that going to be an appropriate response when the child is fifteen and sobbing, too?

If your child/ren are near pubescence or are older, are you ready to talk to them about sex? If you aren't, you need to find someone who is. Don't think your child/ren "wouldn't do that." Given the opportunity, they might. Plan ahead. Make sure each child knows about a variety of birth control methods. Whether or not your child is mentally or physically handicapped in any way can affect whether or not any given method is likely to be effective. Be practical. Be reasonable. Be kind. And don't forget to find out what your state's policies are regarding birth control for foster children.

❧ NOTES ☙

34. Happenstances

Failed Mediation

*Many special-needs children are unable to function normally in the larger world, but **can** be successful within a controlled environment. Some require strict structure to reduce anxiety – precisely the same activity, every day, at the same time. Others just need their world to be limited, going to only a few places, interacting with a small number of people, and participating in only a handful of different activities. Still others can get along fine out in the world as long as there are few expectations of their behavior – they can easily go to church or school, for instance, as long as everyone there is able to tolerate their occasional outbursts.*

*Many children have an appearance that reminds the world of their special needs. This can be excruciatingly painful for them but can also serve a purpose. Others look on the outside as though they are entirely normal, and sometimes that actually makes their lives **more** difficult. It is hard to remember not to give an ordinary looking diabetic child a piece of birthday cake along with the rest of the crowd. When a child with hypertension looks like all the rest of the kids at the sleepover, it is harder to convince the hosts that they really should not be feeding him stuff with all that salt in it. If children with PTSD look normal, it is unlikely that someone who doesn't know them well will recognize the importance of not doing anything that might accidentally be startling or frightening. In a moment, all your best strategies to help your child/ren succeed can go up in smoke.*

Sometimes, no matter what we try, our attempts to control our children's environment are thwarted by other's good intentions. A well-meaning passerby can do damage in an instant that could take years to repair. When that happens, all we can do is pick up and move on, and remember what happened when we plan for the next time.

One of the things about having Posttraumatic Stress Disorder is that you don't like people to touch you without your permission. Even though he has lived with us for fifteen years, the people in Shane's family still don't touch him unless we have his permission. Unfortunately, not everyone is as sensitive.

One morning at church, an acquaintance who worked as a mediator decided to intervene when the boys were horsing around. If he had just spoken to them about it, it might not have been so bad, but he didn't stop there. Though the boys were only playing, he made the mistake of taking it upon himself to grab Shane. It was a big mistake.

Most folks at church had never seen Shane explode like he did that day. Even for those who had, it had been years, because by that time Shane had not fallen apart at church for a long time. He kicked over chairs, and started yelling and pacing. Trying desperately to control himself, what he really wanted to do was beat the guy to a pulp.

The mediator, believing himself to be a good guy, was just trying to help and was oblivious to the fact that he was responsible for Shane's eruption. He kept standing around talking to people, while Shane continued to escalate. Just looking at the guy was infuriating him. Shane became increasingly upset, while I just kept placing myself between them, walking back and forth in time with Shane, hoping I could talk him into calming down before any permanent damage was done.

Eventually, in desperation, I yelled at the guy to *please leave*, which he did. Once he was out of eyesight, Shane was finally able to begin to slow down. It was a relief. The man could easily have ended up in the emergency room, and Shane could have ended up in jail.

No matter how hard we have worked to control Shane's environment so that he has the greatest chance to succeed, sometimes you just can't make enough allowances for the ignorance of others, especially others who mean well.

••

Consider…

What interventions would make it easier for your child to be successful at work, at school, or out in the world?

How can you let others know what your child needs without causing humiliation?

How can you prepare your child for the likelihood that folks in the world will not always respect the same boundaries that your family honors?

What can be done to develop your child's ability to be flexible and to roll with the punches that the world delivers?

What can you do to take care of yourself when accidents happen, your children desperately need you, and internally you're falling apart?

NOTES

35. Catastrophe

Why Not Me?

*Reactive Attachment Disorder is a diagnosis that often results from the circumstances leading to a child's being placed in foster care or for adoption. Agencies may tell you that due to the lack of care given to an infant or toddler prior to the age of eighteen months, the child fails to develop the ability to bond or to attach in any way to others. Once that small window of opportunity is closed, it seems to be virtually impossible for a child to develop the ability at a later time. What agencies don't tell you is what that **means**.*

What it means is that you will never be able to use rewards to get your child to comply with your wishes or expectations, because children with Reactive Attachment Disorder don't care about rewards. You will never be able to get your child to do things just because they are the right things to do, because they don't care about right and wrong. No matter how much or how long you love your child, you will never be able to get your child to be spontaneously kind or loving to anyone else or to any thing, because they don't care about anyone or anything. Consequences and punishment will unfortunately be about the only tools in your toolbox when parenting these kids.

Children with Reactive Attachment Disorder, because they have never learned to bond to others, are completely unable to identify with how their actions affect others. This means they can be cruel to anyone or any creature without feeling any remorse at all. They can lie without shame while looking sweetly into your face. They can break or steal things without any regret whatsoever, all because they are totally incapable of caring about others' feelings. They do not develop a conscience, and almost always grow up to develop into sociopaths. These children become excellent manipulators, and will primarily become interested in figuring out ways to put out the least amount of effort necessary in order to con others into doing what they want. These are the children whose crimes you read about in the paper after they become adults.

*When Brock first came to live with me, I knew he had been diagnosed with Reactive Attachment Disorder. I did not fully appreciate what that would mean for us, however, until after he had already been in my home for a couple of weeks. I don't even remember what had happened now, except that when I asked Doc how to deal with it he looked at me and said, "When dealing with Brock, you are going to have to forget everything you have ever learned about parenting. The ONLY things that are going to work with him are force and coercion." I had no idea at the time how true that would be. I mean, I **really** had no idea.*

Sometimes we have no prior inkling of the catastrophes that are about to hit our families. We're going along, thinking we know what is real and what is not, when suddenly we are taken by surprise. I guess that's why they call things crises. If we knew how to plan for them, they'd never get to that point.

A double dose of one tragic heartbreak to hit our family was brought to light after Brock was sent to a treatment facility because of the harm he was doing to the rest of us. Even though *having* Reactive Attachment Disorder was not his fault, he had become so violent that he was hurting both pets and humans on a regular basis. I could no longer rationalize that maybe, if I just hung in there long enough, we might be able to make life better at home without resorting to more drastic intervention.

Brock had not been in the facility long when I received a call at work asking for permission to take him to the local emergency room in the town where the facility was located. When I asked why, I was told that it was possible that several days before he had been sexually assaulted by an older youth. The staff did not believe it, and they wanted a physical exam to find out. In all fairness, I was furious. I refused to cooperate with the facility's plan, which seemed inadequate at best. Because I worked in a social services agency, I knew that there was a much kinder option for children than hospital emergency rooms. I told the caller that I would not give the permission she wanted and informed her that I was coming immediately to get my son and that I would personally take him to Our Kids, where sexual abuse examinations of children are their specialty.

It was almost the end of the school day, so I picked up Jacob and Shane from school and then drove straight to the facility, where I was told this story: another student had reported that several days before, between the nightly bed-checks by the staff, he had witnessed Brock being assaulted by an older roommate. When the staff had interviewed Brock about the incident, he was told to sit cross-legged on the ground. When he did so, he was told they did not believe that it had happened, because *if* it had he wouldn't have been able to sit that way. They also told him they did not believe that *if* it had happened he was an unwilling participant, because in his fear he did not cry out for help. When he told them he wanted his mother and asked them to call me, they refused. Not only that, but then the staff of the facility let several days pass without making the legally mandated referral to the state's sexual abuse investigation team, and had only called me that morning because another child had told a visitor, who immediately *had* made the legally mandated report and the police were on the way. All of these statements were later verified through their own written case notes.

I was horrified. I had sent my child to a treatment facility out of desperation to keep the rest of the family safe, and there he had not only been assaulted by another child, but also emotionally abused by the staff of the agency. I removed Brock from the program, and we both got back into the car with his waiting brothers. Together, the four of us headed towards the Our Kids clinic in our hometown. It was as we were on the way there, talking in the car about what happened, that I discovered how extensive the catastrophe really was.

As Brock told what happened and how it made him feel, Shane fell silent. Some years before he had benefited from going to the wilderness program, he, too, had gone to a locked treatment facility because of his violent behavior. It had been halfway across the state and he had hated every minute of it, but I had been desperate to find a way to keep him safe. At the time, keeping him in a locked facility until his meds could be regulated had been the only option we could find. During the months that he was there, he had repeatedly told both Doc and myself that he hated it and wanted to come home, but in all fairness, he felt that way about church, school, and the doctor's office, too.

Finally, he spoke. "Why did you get Brock when you didn't come get me?" I asked what he was talking about. "I kept telling you I hated it in Memphis, and you didn't come get me. Why didn't you come get me?" I explained that there was a difference in just not liking a place and what had happened that week to Brock. "But it *is* the same. You *knew*. I *told* you. Why didn't you come get *me*?"

Terror struck deep into my heart as it dawned on me what he was saying. I asked if he was telling me he had been assaulted in Memphis. "I *told* you I hated it there," was all he replied. Desperately, I searched my memory. Yes, he had said he hated it, but neither Doc nor I had any idea *that's* what he had meant. I answered that he always said he hated it everywhere that wasn't home. I said I had not come and gotten him because I had never known he was being hurt there. "You did so know, *I told you. I told you I hated it there.* So why did you take Brock away from the people who were hurting him? *Why not me?*"

• •

Consider…

There is simply no way to prepare for the unexpected heartbreaks and disasters that parenting any child – whether it is a child who is biologically ours, fostered or adopted, or with no attachment to us at all – can sometimes bring. We cannot know what will happen in the future. We cannot know for sure what the ramifications will be of decisions we have made with the best possible intentions. Sometimes the best we can do is to have a good backup plan. What is yours?

✑ NOTES ✑

36. SAFETY

Only Our Own Idiot Doctor Will Do

*"Who will keep me safe?" is one of life's basic questions, along with things like, "What will I eat today?" and, "Where will I sleep tonight?" For children who grow up in safe homes, safety is something like elevator music – there in the background taken for granted unless something happens to bring it to their attention. But for kids who have ended up in foster care and are waiting, either hoping someday to go home again or someday to have an adoptive family of their own, it is right in the forefront all the time. Who **will** keep me safe? And how can I believe it?*

Shane has always refused to talk to any of the doctors on call except his own. As he put it to one of them one day, he didn't want to talk to any of those other idiot doctors. He wanted his own idiot doctor! And no one else would do.

One day, when I had gone down to the drugstore to fill his prescriptions, he decided to try to call them. Neither Jeri nor Doc, both of whose numbers were on our auto-dialer, was available at the time of his call. Instead, the on-call doctors called back. Shane, of course, refused to talk to them, and hung up. They called back. He hung up again. Over and over again it happened.

Someone at Doc's office let him in on what was happening, so he tried calling Shane back, but by then Shane was hanging up every time the phone rang. He never even knew it was Doc on the phone. Doc just kept on trying, but the doctor on call for Jeri had no idea what was going on and called the police.

By the time I got back from the drug store half a block away, Shane was in the back of a police car that was parked in front of our house. As soon as I drove up, an officer came to my car and asked if I had Shane's meds, reassuring me that Shane wasn't in trouble or danger, they were just concerned. Yeah. Me, too.

Sometimes, I wish life with Shane were easier, just a little less complicated, just a little more normal. Sometimes, though, I just have to agree with him. Sometimes, no one but your own idiot doctor will do!

Consider...

What would you need to do to make your home a safer, more stable environment for a child who desperately needs safety and stability?

Think back to a time in your life when you felt in danger. Looking back on it now, were you really unsafe, or were your thoughts what made you afraid?

Sometimes, when fears are more nebulous than, "There's something under the bed," it can help if we speak concretely about what is happening in the moment. "You are safe now." "No one is hurting you now." "I am here now." Has that kind of reassurance ever worked for you, or did you need safety to be demonstrated or proven? How? Would the arms of someone bigger and stronger holding you be sufficient? Would you need someone to actually show you that there's really nothing under the bed?

Safe people are both reliable and reasonable. How can you demonstrate to child/ren who have no reason to believe you that you are a safe person to be around? How long are you willing to wait for them to believe it?

What can you do to help your child/ren discern which other people might be safe, too?

ಐ NOTES ಲ

37. Medication

Gratitude

*Because of their higher incidence rate of mental illness, many foster and adopted children will need psychotropic medications for one symptom or another. Others will need medications for a variety of physical illnesses. In either of these cases, it is impossible to overstress the importance of giving these medications **exactly** as prescribed. Exactly **when** prescribed. Exactly **in the amount** that is prescribed. **Exactly**.*

When a child sees a number of practitioners for a variety of problems, coordinating all of these medications will take a little work. Make sure that each physician knows what all the others have prescribed, the dosage, and directions. Your pharmacist, who will probably get to know you well, can help by making sure that nothing interacts adversely with anything else. For this reason it is important that insofar as it is possible, all prescriptions should be filled at the same pharmacy. The store computer will help keep track of drug interactions for you.

*Don't make **any** changes without talking it over with your child's doctors first. Whether you think a child is having an allergic reaction or is taking too much or too little, it only takes a few minutes to call the office and speak to a nurse or to call the pharmacist with your question. If no one else is available, most poison control hotlines are open twenty-four hours a day.*

*Keep all medications in a locked cabinet to reduce the chances a child will get into them at the wrong time. And did I remember to say to follow directions **exactly**?*

Just the right drug at just the right time can be a wonderful thing. When Shane had to have his wisdom teeth removed, we were very concerned that he needed to be sedated enough to get him home and into a familiar environment before the meds wore off.

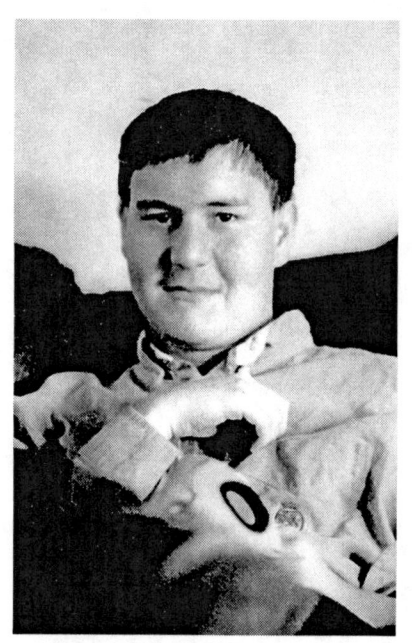

The dentist was great; the prescriptions were given and filled in advance. All we needed Shane to do was wake up enough that we could get him into the car. The trip home would take about half an hour, so time was of the essence.

Everything went off like clockwork. He was almost all the way into his seat in the car before he had second thoughts and staggered back towards the building. Bloody gauze hanging out of his mouth, drool dripping down his chin and heavily drugged, he insisted on going back into the office. Once in, he wanted to see the dentist. All I could think was *Oh, no. What now?*

When the dentist came out, Shane grabbed him by the hand, and started pumping it up and down. "Thank you," he gurgled. "You were wonderful. I didn't feel a thing!" Then he staggered back out to the car where he fell immediately asleep, and away we went.

You just never want to miss an opportunity to say thanks.

Consider…

Find out whether it will be your insurance or the state's that pays for your child's medications. How about deductibles and co-pays? Do you have a place where you can lock meds up, or do you need to go ahead and do something now to prepare for that eventuality?

What would it take to schedule your lifestyle to make sure your child/ren get their meds by the clock?

NOTES

38. CREATIVITY

Alternative Celebrations

*Unusual children frequently call for alternative celebrations of one kind or another. Sometimes that is because it is the occasions that are unusual (How many families do **you** know who celebrate a teenager learning to walk or read?) and sometimes it is because the children themselves know they are not going to get to celebrate the usual milestones in the usual way. As they watch their classmates and friends pass certain landmarks, their inability to do the same can be excruciatingly painful. Something extraordinary needs to be created especially for them.*

As Shane's 18th birthday approached, we began to plan how to mark the day. 16 had come and gone without the trademark driver's license, which we knew he would never be able to have, and we wanted to find some way to make this one special. Even if he always remained a child at heart, on this day, at least, he would be an adult by law.

One way we celebrated the day was to have a state picture ID made. While it may not have been a driver's license, at least it looked like one. Taking the ID with us, we also made the trip down to register him to vote, another thing you couldn't do till you were 18. So, by the end of the day, he had what looked like a driver's license, and a voter's registration card. Not bad for one day.

That night, we celebrated Shane's emancipation the way we celebrated all his birthdays. The one remaining vestige of "McDonald's Therapy" was to always schedule his birthday dinner on the Thursday night closest to his actual birthday. That way, during the time of our regularly scheduled appointment, Doc could join us. Doc's attendance was of ultimate importance to Shane, who was willing to go to any length to make sure dinner was scheduled so that he could attend.

That year, in honor of the occasion, the crowd was larger than usual. Even Jeri came to celebrate with us the miracle that we had made it so far. Shane, with his new ID, was 18 and old enough to smoke but not drink, and wanted cigars to celebrate. I was not about to tell him he couldn't have them, but the cigars I got were blue candy from the local hospital gift shop which read, "It's a boy." Shane laughed aloud at the sight of them, and happily passed them out, making sure everyone in attendance got one. It was a blast.

Another thing we had been working on for quite some time was trying to help him feel independent. Knowing he would not likely leave home for many years, one thing we thought of was getting him his own "apartment." We were able to locate a small office building (12x16 feet) that needed to be moved from its location. Purchasing it and giving him his own room in our backyard would also serve the additional purpose of making it possible for Brock and Jacob to each have separate rooms in the house.

Gifts from family and friends raised the money needed to make the purchase, and the building, which was already paneled, carpeted, and wired for heating and cooling, was transported by truck to its new home. Even though it was parked only a few feet outside the kitchen window (looking out over the site where he had once cooked possum stew), Shane thought it was a grand apartment. The problem was, he was afraid to stay overnight in it. Occasionally, the boys would camp out in it with him, or he would drag the dogs out there to sleep on the nights he dared to stay outside by himself. Many nights, I would wake up to discover him on the couch, or sleeping on the floor outside my door. If the building had not been inside the six-foot wooden fence surrounding the back yard, it might never have happened, but slowly he got used to it.

His biggest problem with it was that he was afraid of tornadoes. Ever since one hit our house several years ago, tornadoes have been his biggest fear. From that day to this, he has wanted an underground room, and his portable building was not in any way, shape, or form underground. Eventually, when the weather started to warm, the three boys started a project designed to fill this need: they were going to dig Shane a basement under his room. The hole did eventually get to be about three feet in diameter, and about as deep, but they never even got far enough along with it so that it reached under the building at all. It was a great idea, anyway.

● ●

Consider…

You've heard the expression, "thinking outside the box." This is a little different. Imagine there is no box. There is no standard you have to meet. Let your imagination run wild. What could you possibly find to celebrate in your child's life? How would you like to do it? What's keeping you from it? When are you going to start?

NOTES

39. Independence

I Just Don't Trust People!

Helping any child gain independence is a struggle. You have all the usual tensions between freedom and responsibility, longing for safety and leaving home. But with special-needs children, both foster and adopted, the spectrum of independence issues is even more intense.

*Even in the best of circumstances, how **does** one get both child and parent ready? Parents, whose lives frequently revolve around even "normal" children, typically struggle with their own longings. They want their children to continue to follow the house rules and to be there when they want them to be there, but they also long for the freedom that independence will grant **them**. Parents may have been living under the stress of caring for a child's special needs for a long time. Part of them wants it to be over, but another part dreads the emptiness of the schedule and the house. Special-needs children, on the other hand, have a whole host of other difficulties. They want to go and they want to stay, sure, but what about the practical issues? Can they reasonably go to college or technical school? Do they need vocational rehabilitation? Will an independent living program be a necessary next step? Are they going to have to stay at home and follow your rules even after they are grown? Are they going to be able to make you change the rules?*

• •

The struggle to help Shane learn to be independent was further hampered by the fact that he had no transportation. He could not drive and never would be able to do so, and he adamantly refused to take the bus. Finally, Earline volunteered to try to teach him how to ride it.

For weeks, she rode the bus to his high school, met him there after school, and showed him how to make the changes to get home. For weeks, he hated every minute of it. There were, after all, people on the bus. Lots of people. They were people on the bus he did not know, and Shane did not like people he did not know.

Finally, on what became the very last day the attempt was made, Shane turned in anguish and blurted out to the person sitting next to him – someone he had never seen before and would never see again: "It's not that I don't trust *you*. I just don't trust PEOPLE."

We let him out of his misery, and never made him try it again.

• •

Consider…

Somehow, your children will have to survive once you are gone, and it is your job to prepare them for that time. What issues do you anticipate arising for *you* as you ready to let your children go?

What was it like leaving home in your family of origin? What is your "best case scenario" for the children you parent? How about the worst?

What obstacles are currently between your child/ren and independence? What will it take to remove them? Who can help you?

NOTES

40. Patience

How Did He DO That?

With special-needs children, you can expect everything to take a little longer. Okay, a lot longer. I once heard that it takes approximately two years of permanency to make up for every year a child has spent in foster care. If that is true, then the older your child/ren are when you get them, the longer and harder the road ahead of you is likely to be. Patience. Patience. Patience.

Within a few months following his 18th birthday, Shane had his first major accident. It was close to the end of the school year, time for his annual meltdown, and he was even more fragile than usual because his psychologist, Doc, had been out of town. Every time Shane missed appointments with Doc, we knew we were in trouble.

On this day he finally erupted, punched out some windows, and cut himself badly. Fearing that he would have to go to jail for breaking the windows, he fled. I could not catch him, and he left a trail of blood.

In desperation, I called the police – his worst fear – but I did not know how else to find him. The police officer who arrived first argued that Shane was 18 years old, and there was nothing they could do because he was an adult. I begged them to understand that he functioned on the level of a second grader. Please, please, I begged, would they help me?

Several phone calls to doctors and superiors later, they agreed. The call went out, and police cars started looking for him. There was a lot of blood, and we did not know how badly he was hurt. By the time it was all over, thirteen police cars and a helicopter were involved in the search. Finally, someone reported seeing him, and he was picked up.

The police transported him to Vanderbilt Hospital, a place he knew well, and I raced over as quickly as I could. By the time I got there, the doctors were desperate. Shane was still bleeding profusely, but he could not read the papers they wanted him to sign, and he was afraid. He would not sign anything, and without his signature, they couldn't do anything.

When I arrived with insurance cards, it still didn't make any difference. Even though he was barely 18 and was essentially incompetent, he was still at that point legally an adult. He wasn't going to sign anything he couldn't read, and he wouldn't let them touch him. I was unsuccessfully pleading with him to let them treat him when much to my relief I got a call from Doc. Doc had literally just gotten back from out of town and had heard about the problem from the on-call doctor. Within minutes, he came to hospital and was able to convince Shane that it was safe to sign the papers, that the people there were safe, and that it was safe to get stitched up. And then he stood by and waited while it was done.

The doctor and the hospital staff were astonished. The question I remember them asking, still, was, "How did he DO that?" What they had no way of appreciating was that it hadn't just taken Doc a little over eight *minutes* to talk Shane into it. It had taken him a little over eight *years*.

■ ■

Consider...

An old adage goes that you should be careful what you pray for, because you just might get it. This is no easy answer: parent one of these children and you're going to need it, so pray for patience, anyway.

NOTES

41. Emancipation

You Never Know

In some cases, no matter how hard you and your children have tried, independence is never going to be an option. What do you do, then, when your children are legally adults but are not mentally so? How about when they do not have the capacity for physically caring for themselves? When they will need some kind of care for the rest of their lives?

For some special-needs children, these arrangements will consist of making plans for physical accommodations. These children may have the mental capacity to function as adults, but have some physical limitation that needs to be addressed. Perhaps they need a home and job with handicap accessibility. Maybe they need a large screen monitor and visual enhancement program so they can work on the computer at home. It could be they will need an apartment on a bus line, or an independent living program of one kind or another. They may be able to be self-supporting either with or without additional financial assistance such as Food Stamps or Section 8.

*Still other children have mental handicaps that prohibit them from self-care. These children may be **willing** to take their medications, for instance, but have no idea what day of the week it is or if they already remembered to take their meds today or not. For this type of child, a med box is not going to help. S/he will actually need someone to hand them any medication when it is time. The child may be unable to dress, or bathe, much less support him or herself financially. These children may need someone to fill out applications for programs such as Disability or SSI for them, or have a legal guardian appointed for their own protection.*

••

For the next two years, I tried to get conservatorship of Shane. I worried constantly that another accident would happen, and sure enough, two years later, it did. We were once again approaching the end of the school year. Change was in the works, and Shane has never done well with change.

Although at twenty years old Shane had struggled for a long time to complete his graduation requirements, we already knew he was not going to be able to get a regular diploma. He had hung in there until he accumulated all of the credits required for a special education diploma, but he had never been able to pass the TCAP, the eighth grade equivalency exam required to get a regular diploma in the state of Tennessee. He was disappointed and frustrated. Still, he finally agreed to participate in walking through the line at graduation, on the condition that Doc would come stand in line with him.

His anxiety level continued to climb the closer we got to the end of the year. Finally, the week before graduation, he snapped. We had just moved and I was trying to force a new stove through a too-small door into the kitchen, when it got stuck in the doorway. Shane came in to talk to me and I told him I could not talk just then, and to go to his room to cool off. It was more than he could bear. Once again, he started punching windows. Once again, he began to bleed.

This time, though, it was terrifying. He cut through an artery in two different places. Blood was spurting from his wounds, more blood that I could remember ever having seen in real life, and I knew that there would be no way to get him into in an ambulance with people he did not know.

We were able to wrestle him into the car, using a belt as a tourniquet, and began the race to the hospital not knowing if he would even let them touch him once we arrived. I honestly believed he would bleed to death before we got there. My hope was that he would be passed out by the time we made it, and they would be able to stitch him up before he came to.

Since we had recently moved, we were headed to a hospital we were unfamiliar with and where he would not feel safe. Success was unlikely. A police officer saw us speeding and started to chase us a few blocks before the hospital. We didn't even slow down.

By the time we got to the hospital, even Shane believed he was going to die, and he began weeping and wailing like a small child. "I want my mother," he kept crying. "I want to see my mother before I die." We rushed him into the emergency room, and when the officer who was following us saw the blood all over Shane, all over the inside of the car, and all over us, he didn't even stop us. "Just call an ambulance next time," he said, not knowing why we hadn't called one in the first place.

Shane's arms were cut so badly this time that they couldn't even stitch him up at the small county hospital where we went, though they were able to get the bleeding to stop. He was frightened enough by then that he agreed to let them drug him a sufficient amount to transport him in an ambulance, this time back to Vanderbilt, where once again they sewed him back together.

I had been afraid that he would die. He had been afraid he would die. And he almost did. They said at the county hospital that the only reason he had not died was that he was so strong, the very strength that had been wearing me out for years. The best part of the whole drama was that as a result of the accident, a kind Vanderbilt law professor named Julie Sandine stepped in and facilitated the resolution of Shane's interminable conservatorship proceedings, so that I would never again be in the position of not being able to sign in order to get him the help he needed. You just never know what will happen, or what good might come of it in the end.

∙ ∙

Consider…

What kinds of provisions are your children likely to need made for them? Not just insurance or money – every child or young adult needs that. What other needs are your *specific* children going to experience? How can *those* needs be addressed once your child/ren are no longer in your care?

What do you need to start doing now in order to help make success possible for them later?

❧ NOTES ☙

42. Reunions

Pomp and Circumstances

Virtually all foster and adopted children long for their families of birth. They want to know why their mother didn't love them, because they think she must not have if she gave them up. They wonder if they have their father's eyes, or their grandparent's smile. They fret about what they must have done wrong to make their own families hate them. They ache to know if they have brothers and sisters who think and feel just like them. It is for reasons like these that even grown children search for their families of birth. It is not because they do not love you or are ungrateful. It is because they are human.

No matter how painful it may be initially – either for them or for their foster/adoptive parents – many of these concerns can be ameliorated by simple contact with the birth family. A lot of the time, it is just plain better to know than not to know. Know, and you only have to deal with the truth. Not know, and you worry forever over every imaginable possibility.

As a result of the accident, it became my mission to find Shane's mother for him. When he thought he was dying, finding her was all he wanted; and so, loving him, I wanted that for him, too.

Shane and his biological siblings, although they had not seen their mother in about fifteen years, had always kept in contact with each other. Shane's little brothers often came to our house to visit or he went to theirs, and his little sister even went to his high school. In fact, she was going to graduate with a regular diploma on the very same day Shane received his special education diploma.

After all the adoptive parents involved talked about it and agreed with the plan, one of the twins was able to locate their birth mother on the Internet and invite her to the graduation. Although none of us knew for sure if she would actually come, the parents were planning for a reunion without telling Shane. All Shane knew was that we were planning a party.

For three of his high school years, Shane had taken Chef Campbell's cooking classes as electives. He loved the classes, although he hated washing dishes. His specialty was making the cornbread for the weekly lunch the students cooked for the teachers on Wednesdays. Chef had a small Tea Room in which the teachers ate, and she graciously agreed to cater a party for his graduation.

On the day of graduation, Shane was mighty nervous. Wearing long sleeves to hide the bandages still covering his arms, he put on his robe and stood anxiously in line – watching, and watching, and watching for Doc. When Doc finally arrived, I took off to join the others in the stands. And there, sure enough, was Shane's mom. I had not seen her since before I knew he would be mine, while I still worked for CASA and she was at some juvenile court proceeding, but I recognized her right away. It was an amazing experience to sit with her as she watched two of her children, whom she had not seen in over a dozen years, graduate from high school.

The twins and their dad had picked her up, but Shane and Tasha were already among the graduates on the field and did not yet know that she had come. The plan was for all the families to meet in the Tea Room afterwards. Not until all arrived did Shane know she was actually there.

The twins were there with their adoptive family. Tasha was there with hers. We were there with all of ours. And Sandra was there, for the first time since the children were preschoolers, with all of the children she had given up years before in order to protect them from their abuser.

It was the sort of moment they make movies about. Shane had a red rose in his hands, for all the seniors had been given one, and in the most tender gesture you can imagine he walked up to the mother he had not seen since he was five years old, and offered her the rose which was all he had to give. There wasn't a dry eye in the room. It was one of the sweetest things I have ever had the privilege of witnessing.

Consider...

What is the *worst* thing that could happen if your child searched for his or her birth family? Would it be worse to find them, or not to find them? Are you afraid your child/ren would want to leave you? Do you realistically think they would?

What is the *best* thing that could happen if your child found his or her birth family? Would it be worth the risk of the worst possibility you just thought of? Is it important enough to your child/ren that you are willing to help them try?

NOTES

43. Disruption

When Termination Comes before You're Ready

*Although we always hope our children will be with us until it feels right to **us** for them to go, sometimes that is not possible. In the case of foster children, we have no power at all over decisions made about them. **All** of their possibilities lie in someone else's control. In some states, after a foster child has been with you for a year they are at least supposed to **consider** your input, but in the end it is the state or agency who placed them with you, and it is the state or agency which can take them away. If you're lucky, you have enough lead-time to say goodbye and prepare. If you're not so lucky, you can only grieve after they are gone.*

With adoptions, too, sometimes termination comes before we're ready. Some adoptions, like some pregnancies, are terminated before they have come to fruition. Sometimes, with some children, you just can't make things work no matter what you do. Some children's needs are too great, some are too sick, and some are too violent or damaged for an individual family to be able to help them. In some circumstances you may be able to place a child in a facility that will allow you to retain parental rights, but in other cases it is necessary to actually place the child back into state custody in order to get him or her the services that are needed. Either case feels like tragedy.

Once upon a time, I had a foster child who was removed from my home before I was ready. She had already lived with me for just over eleven months when the state, in its infinite wisdom, placed her with an uncle to whom they would not have to make foster care payments. I was devastated. I did not believe it was in my child's best interest, and years later I learned I was right. After her eighteenth birthday she came back and found me again, and told me her uncle had sexually abused her for years. I swore I would never put myself in that position again, and resolved never again to foster another child. I was wrong. I did foster again, anyway. It is no child's fault that the system itself is faulty.

Almost exactly twenty-five years later, our family experienced another disruption. This time it was my choice. Again, I was not ready. Although I did not want to do it, this time I was the one who made the difficult choice to place Brock back into state custody three months before his eighteenth birthday. Our family was not safe from him, and he was too large for me to contain him. After multiple attempts to get the state to pay for the services he had been promised at the time of his adoption, it all came down to one day in court when it became clear that as long as he was in my custody they were not going to provide what he needed. They didn't have to, and they weren't going to. Only if he was returned to their custody would he be placed somewhere that both he and the rest of the family could be safe. I had to choose.

In the balance were Shane and Jacob. They were both at great risk. Because of Jacob's Polycystic Kidney Disease, his danger was that Brock would hit him in such a way that he would bleed to death internally before we could get him to a hospital.

Shane's peril was of a different sort. Brock would emotionally torture Shane, doing things like choking Shane's dog in front of him in an attempt to get Shane, who was by that time legally an adult, to hit him. The danger was that since Shane was an adult, he might end up in jail. Neither was a chance I was willing to continue to take.

Putting Brock back into state custody meant having to deal with all of Shane's fear of abandonment again. If I would do it to Brock – even to protect the rest of the family – in Shane's thinking there was nothing to keep me from doing it to him. And I also had to deal with my own feelings about what my failure to be able to get one of my children launched into adulthood said about me. It was the act of surrendering custody itself that felt like I had violated everything I had ever promised the boys.

Though my parental rights were not terminated (I even had to pay the state child support and continue to pay for Brock's medical insurance during the time he was in state care) I felt as though I had failed in my promise and my goal. I wasn't ready, because I didn't think he was ready. I cried, as they say, a river. But I did what I believed needed to be done in the best interest of the entire family.

•••

Consider…

Foster care and adoption carry different risks. On the one hand, inherent in foster care is the presupposition that the child is not legally yours. You have no power of decision making, but neither do you have the financial responsibility either. When you have adopted a child, on the other hand, you have both the freedom to make choices and the bottom line responsibility for the child's care – no matter what the contract says. In the end, if the state doesn't pay for a service your child needs, you foot the bill. Each of these types of care carries with it its own risks. No one but you can decide which is preferable. In your circumstance, is it better to have less power but more financial freedom? Or is it better to have both control and fiscal responsibility?

Each relationship also contains within the possibility for disruption before you are ready. Is it worth it to you?

✺ NOTES ✺

44. Vulnerability

Used and Abused

Children who are fragile are easier for the world to take advantage of. Especially in school situations, they may be used or abused by their classmates. Smaller children have their money or lunches stolen. Children who are different are picked on. Children who are trusting are used to others' advantage. But school is not the only place that happens. Children who have been previously physically or sexually abused are more vulnerable to those things happening again. It is not possible for us as parents to protect our children everywhere or at every time. Whether birth, foster, or adopted, sometimes the best we can do is to help our children process what has happened and think through what might make the outcome different if something like that happens again in the future.

Shane had continued to volunteer for Lynn in the adult day program throughout the rest of high school. Each day, multiple times a day, he would remind himself that the agency director had promised him a job if he just finished high school, and he had stayed in school long after he could have dropped out because he *really* wanted that job. He had forced himself to go to classes in the high school building based on that promise, and had eventually forced himself to leave the self-contained classroom altogether to go into the resource classrooms so that he could take even more classes. *Everything* he did for the last two years of high school was based on the promise of getting a job doing what he loved.

After graduation, Shane was inconsolable when he discovered that the director of the agency where the adult day care was did not intend to give him a job after all. After all the work he had done to graduate, and after they allowed him to volunteer there for two additional years believing that he would be given a paying job once he finished, the director had Lynn's supervisor tell the three of us that they were not going to give Shane the job he had been promised. She said it was because they really wanted someone with a driver's license. That was something we knew that Shane would never have.

I was furious. They had used him for the previous two years, apparently, with no intention of actually hiring him. They had given him an award for being a volunteer, and even said they wanted him to keep volunteering. But they were not going to give him a way to support himself. He was heartbroken. He kept trying to figure out what he had done wrong.

No matter how much we tried to help him understand that it was not anything he had done, it did not help. Finally, Shane took the grief over his disappointment and turned it around. For almost three years, his only goal had been to graduate from high school in order to get the job that he wanted. Now, even knowing that because he would never have a driver's license no diploma would ever be enough, he would keep going. He had a special education degree, but he decided he would never give up until he got a regular high school diploma.

Consider...

What is your history of being used/abused/taken advantage of by larger, older, more powerful, or more experienced people in your life? At home? At school? At work?

What special limitations do your child/ren have that may make them especially vulnerable to any kind of abuse?

How can you prepare them to respond when that happens? In most cases, the safest response is to comply and then tell a reliable adult as soon as possible. While your child may not have the power to keep something from happening to them once, you or someone you know may have the power to keep it from happening to them ever again.

Who can your child talk with to help them make sense of what happened and move on?

NOTES

45. Support Systems

The Most Magnificent Tutor

The demands of special-needs and hard-to-place children are extensive, so their support systems will have to be, too. Some of the roles — doctors and therapists, for instance — will be universal. It is a safe bet that your child is going to need them. Other roles will be specific to your child/ren and their needs: tutors, physical therapists, occupational therapists, speech therapists, or specialists in a variety of medical fields. Then there are the people who will fill needs that may not immediately come to mind — like Liz and Nelson at Import Auto Maintenance, who for many years were two of the most important people in our family's support system because they kept my tired old car running. Year after year, they made it possible for me to get the children to whatever school or doctor's appointment was scheduled next; many days, they even loaned me a car when the van with the "I Adopt" license plate wouldn't run at all. The older the car got, the more I needed Nelson and Liz.

You may think you had your support system all lined up before your child came, but as s/he ages, new issues will arise or will mutate out of the old ones. Remain flexible. Ask around. Check the yellow pages. Look on bulletin boards. Call referral services. Continue to gather your support around your family and widen its base if possible. As your children mature, you're going to need all the help you can get.

••

We would never have gotten as far as Shane's decision to work towards a regular high school diploma if it had not been for Sherry Ware. Sherry had taken over as Shane's tutor once he got to her Special Education/Moderate Intervention Program (MIP) Fragile class in junior high. Hers was the class he ended up in when he came back from the wilderness program, and even though it was across town from our house, we had gotten special permission for him to go there so that he would have after school care.

Each day after school, he would walk from Sherry's class to Marvin and Mae Webb's house, two doors down. Granny and Pop served as his surrogate grandparents, and in return, he did anything he could for them. Chores, lifting, carrying, yard work, it didn't matter to him. He loved them both and would do anything they asked. After I got off work, I would haul him over to Sherry's house so that she could tutor him in whatever they were trying to learn that week, and once he got to high school, they would work on his homework.

He always went into Sherry's house looking for Miss Toots, her cat, who couldn't stand him. The cat would hiss at him, but he would look for her anyway, exclaiming, "Oh! The Toots loves me!" If it was true, her love must have been blind, because she never recognized the object of her affection.

One day, after Miss Toots finally died, Sherry was outside raking leaves when Shane came over, and a new cat came and found her. Shane loved that cat, too, even though it always ran when it saw him. Sometimes he and Sherry would work on schoolwork, sometimes they would study for the TCAP, and sometimes Sherry would be amazed when she needed help and Shane would lift heavy things like stone pillars as easily as Sherry could pick up a couch cushion. As she put it, "No matter how heavy things were, he picked them up like they were toothpicks."

After graduation, Shane wanted to take Sherry out to dinner with his graduation money, so she drove him to the closest outlet mall. There, he took her to the food court where he bought her Gyro sandwiches. Then he took what was left of his money and went shopping for his "graduation clothes," all of which he tried on for her before he bought them. She said he would show her what he picked out, rub the fabric, and exclaim, "Good quality!"

Touched by Shane's determination to get a *real* high school diploma, Sherry stepped in when we had no money to continue to pay for tutoring because his adoption assistance ended when he graduated from high school. She volunteered to keep tutoring him for free because she had never known a child who tried harder. For the next two years, until they gave the TCAP for the very last time, she made good on her promise and tutored him at least two times every single week. If he was going to make it, she would be the reason why.

Consider…

There will be days when the closer you get to your goal of getting your foster and adopted child/ren grown, the farther away it will seem. This is not the time to give up. What supports does your family need *now*? Where can you find them? Who and what can sustain *you*?

NOTES

46. Focus

Practice Makes Perfect

*In some respects, the closer you get to the goal, the harder it is to see anything else. At those times you want to keep your goal in mind, but it is still necessary to keep your perspective. Especially when your child may not see anything else at all except the thing that s/he wants, **you** have to keep focus on the larger picture. Sure, you want to be encouraging, but is the world really going to end if the goal is not met? Focusing on one thing at a time may make it possible to break goals into small enough sections to succeed, but no one thing is everything, except in movies or books. Winning is not everything. Success is not everything. Money is not everything. Maybe love. Maybe love is everything. One love at a time. One step at a time. One day at a time. Focus.*

For the next two years, Shane dedicated his life to studying for the TCAP and taking it over and over again every time it was given. Now that they didn't have homework to work on, he and Sherry could just work on that annoying test. They started out by focusing on the math portion, because that was the part he had come closest to passing each time he had taken it. Since he only had to pass each portion once, if he could just pass that part, he could get it out of the way and then just focus on the language, which was infinitely harder for him.

Each time he took the math test he got closer to passing, until finally he was within three points of success. It was excruciating each time, waiting for the results to come back. Should they keep working on math? Should they start the language? Finally, about nine months after graduation they came to the night before it would be given one more time.

Each go around, on the last night before the test, Shane and Sherry would do the same thing: hit the hardest points for one last review, then one last pass through the whole test at once. This time, he had gone over to Sherry's classroom and they were doing one last review of his greatest difficulty, decimals. It was almost impossible for him to master them, because even at twenty-one he still did not know his right hand from his left, so he could never remember in which direction the decimals got larger, and in which direction they got smaller.

Finally, Sherry just lit into him. She said she knew she must have been blue in the face when she exclaimed, "By now even the fish in the fish tank know their decimals!" and she wrote L and R on his hands. Shane responded by getting even madder than she was, and by calling her everything, as she put it, but a child of God. He stomped off down the hall, yelling that he was never coming back. As he stormed away, he was already on his cell phone telling me that he was *quitting*.

In the background, I could hear her still calling out helpful instructions: "OK, get a good night's sleep, take a deep breath, don't forget everything I've taught you." On my end of the phone I wanted to throttle him for not taking advantage of this last night to cram before the exam, while on the other end, Sherry was still calling after him down the hall, "Call me when its over, make sure you eat breakfast, take a snack." All the time she was saying these things to him, he was calling her every name he knew.

The next day, he was still so angry that he raced through the exam and came out in about half the time it usually took him. I was so upset I could hardly speak to him. I was sure he had blown off the test, but when Mr. Kittrell called with the results, he asked if I was sitting down. He said Shane had not just passed the test that day, he had made an unbelievable 84. Sherry said that when Mr. Kittrell called to tell her, they could hear her yelling all over the school.

....

Consider…

What distractions in your life keep you from focusing on your larger goals? TV? Video or computer games? Mindlessly idling away the hours? What is it that you do when you really need to be doing something else? When you *are* doing those things, what is it you are avoiding?

What *are* your goals, anyway? This week? This month? This year? Five years? Ten years?

How does a special-needs child or children fit into that picture?

What example do you want to set about your own priorities?

How can you do it?

NOTES

47. Activities

Buddha, the Dog

Like almost every other kid in the world, special-needs kids just want to be like everyone else their age. They want to be regular, to be normal. They want to have pets, play sports, take lessons, run, walk, swim, read, write, draw, and they want us to help them pull it off. You may find, however that with these children it takes a little more effort and planning than it might require for most other youngsters.

At our house, we've had horses, donkeys, chickens, doves, lovebirds, dogs, cats, rats, snakes and hamsters – a larger number of choices than most families, I guess. Some pets worked for some children and not for others, but still not a single one of my children ever remembered to feed or water their pets unless reminded, and rarely were any of them happy to do so when told.

I've had children who played soccer, swam, ran, rode horses, practiced judo, learned aikido, danced, threw footballs or threw each other, and some of them did all of these things. Some indulged in one sport, some another, some several, and other children participated in none.

Some of my kids loved to draw, others to play instruments in the band, and some wanted nothing more than to sit in front of the computer day after day after day.

And your children will be like that, too. The goal is to find activities for them that they can participate in and be successful. Finding the right pet for the right child may take several tries. A child may need to be unsuccessful at one or more sports before agreeing to try Special Olympics. They may hate being told by their band director to play the trombone, because what they really want to play is drums. In short, special-needs kids are just like us. They have to find the activities that fit and work for them.

• •

Some activities are more successful for some special-needs kids than others, and you never really know which ones are going to work until you have given them a try. Pets, for instance. Ever since Shane was a little boy, he had wanted a basset hound. We had a dozen other dogs at different times, but none of them would do. For my part, the only basset I had ever known was old and very laid-back, so when one of my co-workers had a litter for sale, I thought it would make sense to get him one of the pups. I had no appreciation at the time for the difference in an old, laid-back dog, and what that dog must have been like as a pup. The puppy we got was as wired as it could be.

In fond memory of his trip to Missoula and his love for Noel, who by that time had joined a Buddhist order, Shane named the puppy Buddha, and he loved the dog with all his heart. The dog never stopped moving, but at night Shane would still drag the poor thing to bed with him. When it was morning, they got up together, and he loved that dog all day long. He especially loved the fact that Buddha slobbered, though I have never understood why. For almost ten months, they were completely inseparable. Then, one sad morning, the puppy escaped from the yard. We put signs all over the neighborhood, and looked high and low. Buddha was found, eventually, on the railroad tracks close to our house by one of our neighbors. Shane's heart was completely broken. In spite of that, he did not give up loving animals. Having loved once, he has had two other dogs since: Maxie, who died of old age, and Nika, who currently sleeps upon his bed.

In addition to being a successful pet-owner, Shane has had success with other activities, too; it just took a few tries. He successfully learned to play one basic beginner piece on the piano. It took him an entire school year to do it, but he did. He discovered that he loved to draw – just not to take art lessons – so draw he does. And after several false starts, he actually played a sport in one game. It started because Noel took Judo, so Shane wanted to take Judo. And, of course, he had to study with Noel's Judo instructor, Keo. Unfortunately, Keo may have been an expert at Judo, but he wasn't an expert at teaching any sport to Shane, who was, at that point in his life, quite a handful. Shane may not have been *quite* as wired as Buddha, but he was close. Shane disrupted the classes, so Keo had one of his students teach Shane privately, outside of class. That didn't quite work either.

Eventually, Shane moved on to soccer. Noel played soccer, so Shane wanted to play soccer. The difficulty was multifaceted. Shane seemed to be completely unable to learn the necessary skills – other than kicking the ball, which he loved. And believe me, he could *really* kick that ball! Finally though, when Shane got to high school, we discovered that the school had a Special Olympics soccer team he qualified for. More problems. There are people on soccer teams. Lots of them – players, and coaches, too. People Shane didn't know. And Shane does *not* trust people.

We finally got past that problem, and after many practices at school, it was time for the Special Olympics themselves. That's when the chaos really started. The games were being held in a neighboring town, and the team was required to stay at a hotel. More people. More change. More confusion. More challenges. *Finally*, we got to the first game: Shane running, yelling, "I've got it! I've got it!" Shane kicking the ball – *really* kicking the ball – and his shoe (Remember that he always chose shoes several sizes too large?) accompanying the ball, flying with it half the length of the field. It is the only real game he ever played. He said he would never do it again.

But he did it once. And he is still talking about it. Finding the right activity may take a little time, but the memories are worth it.

• •

Consider...

What difference does it make to you whether or not your child/ren participate in one activity over another?

What do you think it says about *them* as humans and as your children if they persevere versus going on to try something else?

What do you think it says about *you* as a parent? As a person?

What would it take for you to completely let go of those expectations so that your child/ren could just learn something new and have fun?

❧ NOTES ☙

48. SERENDIPITY

He Gets By with a Little Help from His Friends

Life is a mystery, especially when things seem to fall into place of their own accord. We notice it at those times because at other times we plan and scheme only to have everything fall flat. Clearly, we are not in control of our world, of our children, or even of ourselves. To make it through life, each of us needs assistance from time to time. We hope for it. We ask for it. But even then we are not always prepared to accept it when it comes. It is advantageous if we can come to expect the unexpected, learn to roll with the punches, and then be grateful when whatever the future does bring is good. Low expectations. High gratitude. That's the ticket.

Special education students are allowed to take the graduation exams as many times as they need to, for as long as they need to, until they pass. At least, that's the theory. The unfortunate truth is that about two years after Shane graduated, the state decided to change to a different exam. What that meant for students was that after a certain date they would no longer be administering the old test, but would switch to the new one. If Shane did not pass the second half of the exam by the last testing date, he would have to start all over with the new exam, which had four parts instead of two. The task seemed overwhelming.

We were getting more and more panicked. The last three times Shane had taken the language portion of the test, he had made within a point or two of the same score, always just below the passing margin. We began to fear that maybe that was his maximum level, and that he would never make it. All of those who were working with him agreed that if he did not pass the TCAP, it was completely unreasonable to expect him to start over with the Gateway. When it came down to the very last testing date, we knew it was everything or nothing.

Shane's whole life was riding on this one test. No matter how many times Doc or the rest of us told him that we were just as proud of him for trying so long and so hard as we would have been if he had passed, it wasn't what Shane wanted to hear. He wanted a real diploma, and nothing else would do.

The last time he had taken the TCAP he had gotten completely lost on the tape recording he was allowed to use, and had just done the best he could reading the questions for himself. As a result, his score had dropped a few more points. It was bad enough that he couldn't read the test; he couldn't even master the tape recorder, and up until that point he hadn't been allowed to have help.

The night before the test, it was the same ritual as always: studying with Sherry. Going over the worst parts from previous tests, in this case those troublesome homonyms. Then taking the practice test as a whole. A good dinner, a good night's sleep. Eat a good breakfast, take a snack. All we could do was all we could do. After I got him to Mr. Kittrell at the high school, I just went outside and sat in the car and cried. This was it. Everything he had worked so hard on was riding on the next few hours. This was his very last chance.

When he came out after the test, he told me the same story as always, "I think I passed it this time." But then he told me more. A former teacher at the high school who knew he could not master the tape recorder had obtained permission for an aide Shane knew well, trusted, and liked, to read him the test one question at a time so he would not get lost. Mr. Kittrell and the special education resource staff had made sure he got snacks and soft drinks in addition to the ones he brought. They made him take breaks, and pumped up his morale between sessions so that he would not give up.

I was overwhelmed at their kindness. If he did not pass this time, it would certainly not be because they had not done every single thing within their power to help him. Even though he had to be the one to answer the questions on the test, administering it had truly been a group act of love on the part of his friends on the faculty. They gave him the best chance he had ever had.

• •

Consider...

When have you ever been the recipient of an unexpected kindness? What kind of a difference did that experience make in your life? What did it mean to you at the time to be dependent on someone else's charity? How about now?

Even if we want to provide for our children ourselves, no one person or couple can do everything. What obstacles within you make it difficult for you accept that you are finite and limited in what you can do? What do you think it would it say about you if you were unable to personally provide everything your child needs?

What would it take to be ready when the time comes to accept an offering from an outsider on your child's behalf?

NOTES

49. PERSEVERANCE

Just When I Needed It Most

Multitudes of people ranging from Winston Churchill to the Dalai Lama have said something to the effect of, "Never, never, never, never, never give up." But you know, when we're tired, it's just so tempting to say we've done all that we can do. We are human, after all. We get discouraged. We do, in fact, wear out. Oh, yes. These children do wear us out.

The problem with giving up is that then we never find out what might have happened if we had just hung in there a little longer. We never know what difference only one more day might have made. Maybe no more than one more hour would have been all the time it took to change your child's life.

The news finally came while I was praying in the sanctuary at All Saints. It had been a hard year. My marriage had fallen apart. I had lost my job. I was overwhelmed, and was sitting in the quiet sanctuary, praying for relief.

In the midst of my distress, the cell phone rang. It was Mr. Kittrell, wanting to know if I could bring Shane to him. The results had come in. He didn't want me to tell Shane; he wanted to do it himself. It was not long before the end of the school day, so I rushed to where Shane was and picked him up. We headed to the high school, with him becoming more and more suspicious by the minute.

The news, when he finally got it, was surprisingly anticlimactic. The resource staff members were themselves bubbling over with joy, but Shane just sat there, stunned. Mr. Kittrell kept asking him if he understood, and he just kept saying, "Okay." Finally he grinned, but he still kept waiting for the other shoe to fall. Having worked towards this one goal for so long, he seemed at a loss for what to do next. His final score had been an 84, just like on the math.

We headed down the block to the junior high to tell Sherry Ware, who literally went running up and down the halls screaming that he had made it. Then, she ran to the office to tell all of them, too. The office staff had known Shane since he was a student there in junior high, and had seen him daily as he came to get his hall pass to go for tutoring. They, too, joined in the celebration. The tortured hours, the broken furniture, the years of anguish; suddenly it had all been worth it.

Sherry says to this day that she has never been happier in all her life. Considering the despair I was feeling before the phone rang, I know that was true for me, too. The graduate, for his part, was still in shock for months.

It may take Shane a little longer to do things than most people, but time after time he has shown us that there is nothing he cannot do when he sets his mind to it. He is the living embodiment of never give up. *Never give up.* **Never give up.**

Consider…

One suggestion I have heard is that if you need help keeping your life in balance, you should HALT! Don't let yourself get too Hungry, too Angry, too Lonely, or too Tired. When you are any of those things it is too easy to give in or to give up.

What symptoms are your personal danger signs? Too depressed? Too worried? Too broke? How can you protect yourself from failure when you are just plain too worn out?

❧ NOTES ☙

50. Timing

The Nose Knows

*They say that in comedy, timing is everything. That's **not** the only place in life where that is true. Whether you are fostering or adopting special-needs children, the amount of coordination it takes to make all the parts of your day fall into place is overwhelming. Scheduling a day could take an act of congress. Scheduling a week can require a full-time secretary. Problem is, most of us don't have one.*

Like layers of an onion, on most days we just peel away one thing at a time until the next thing to be done reveals itself. Major life events, like surgery, require a skill at organization that a choreographer for an entire dance troupe would envy.

Shane might not have been able to communicate to us much of what happened to him before I got him, but his nose told us a lot. Part of his abuse had been to have his nose broken in several places, and he had never been able to breathe very well. One nostril was completely closed; the other almost so. For years, we had put off the operation to fix it, for fear of his destabilization under anesthesia and the pain of recovery. If the anesthesia made him throw up his psych meds, or the pain triggered his PTSD to any great extent, we knew we'd really be in trouble.

After he finally passed the TCAP, though, we decided to risk it. The nurses and doctors were wonderful. They talked him through everything that was going to happen, and timed the surgery so that he could take all his regular meds. It was a blessing.

Although the ten days following the surgery were anguish for all of those of us who were at home, since Shane could not swallow and was hungry and GROUCHY all the time until he could eat normally again, for the first time he could actually breathe through his nose.

The surgery also opened up the back of his throat, making it possible for him to breathe while he sleeps without sleep apnea waking him up all night long. (A C-PAP breathing machine had been considered for years, but none of us had reason to believe he could master it.) He now has more energy during the day, due to finally (after all these years) being able to sleep better at night, and he's in a little better mood, too. Thank goodness.

Consider...

Some people are innately better at planning than others. It *is*, however, a skill that can be learned. As you look down the road at parenting over the long haul, who is the best planner you know? This may be an excellent time to get them to teach you what they know. If you don't use one already, buy a daily planner and get in the habit of using it. You're going to need it.

NOTES

51. Setbacks

The Bridge

*Many times in your life you may have heard the expression, "One step forward and two steps back." Parenting special-needs kids may not be quite **that** bad, but it is occasionally, "Two steps forward and one step back." No different, in that respect, than life for anyone else.*

Progress is never all one-way. Every single one of us goes back and forth, up and down. The rate of time may be different, or the degree of the angle, but all of us progress at some times and have setbacks at others.

The trick is to have enough experience at failure that we don't get stuck in the mire of the setbacks when they happen. The lesson they offer us is how to pick ourselves up again and move on. Sometimes we teach that skill to our children. Other times they teach it to us.

That summer, on a Thursday, we again hit the difficult time in June when Shane had his annual meltdown. For the first ten years, we thought he fell to pieces at that time of year because he could not handle the transition from school to summer program. Every year like clockwork, within a week or two of the first of June, he would just fall apart. For the first six years he lived with me, he ended up in the hospital every time it came about, just as he did during the break for the Christmas holidays, but each year he got a little better at handling the change. It was only after he finally finished school and still continued to struggle during that time of year that we realized it had more to do with the PTSD than with school. We may never know what that time of year triggers in him, but we do know that any change in his routine is always troublesome.

The year after he finally passed the TCAP exam to get his regular high school diploma was his best yet. He seemed happy and relaxed. He laughed a lot, and seemed to be thinking more clearly than ever before. He started volunteering two days a week at a building materials recycling center, doing whatever he could to be helpful to Jack, the guy who ran the place. They were getting along well and Shane seemed to be more confident every day. Then, on the tenth of June, it all came crashing down.

Shane had been trying to sort hinges. Most days, he had been the strong man, helping to lift, carry, and move anything and everything that no one else could do. He had demolished buildings and moved furniture and appliances, but those little hinges got to him that day. He knew he was supposed to sort them out by size, but he was getting more and more frustrated by the minute. He just could not figure it out. Finally he couldn't contain his frustration any longer. In his anguish, he knocked over eight shelving units, broke two pieces of furniture, a sink and a water heater, and smashed two light fixtures before storming out of the store.

Totally panicked, Jack called me on the phone, "You've got to talk me through this one," he started. While we were talking, he jumped in his truck and started driving in the direction he thought Shane had gone. I raced from my work to my car and started driving to where he thought Shane was heading, hoping to head him off from the opposite direction. I kept talking to Jack all the way until finally, I saw Shane crossing a bridge on foot ahead of me, with Jack following at a safe distance behind. I pulled over to the side, and when Shane got up even with me I got his attention and asked him if he would like a ride. By the time he got in the car, I was handing him his meds and a glass of water.

It turned out he had started walking towards the bridge with the intention of throwing himself off of it, since he was sure his life was over because he thought he would be arrested and sent to jail for breaking things. Fortunately, by the time he reached the bridge, he had calmed down enough that he had decided to keep walking towards our friend Earline's house. That was where he was headed when I happened upon him.

By the time we had driven fifteen minutes, he was already problem solving and had decided to call his psychiatrist, Jeri. The speed of his recovery was remarkable, and a clear indication of how much he had improved. In the old days, his comeback would have taken months.

• •

Consider…

Beating ourselves up over our setbacks doesn't do any of us any good, but almost all of us do it from time to time. Next time you do it, listen to what you are saying to yourself. Are you saying that what you did was terrible or that there is no way to fix it? Is that really true? If not, what *is* the truth? Are you telling yourself that you made a mistake? That you can try again and maybe you'll do better next time? Start by just telling yourself the truth about the action.

Then, think about what you *believe* about yourself as a result of what you tell yourself. Do you believe that you're horrible or bad? It is not likely true that you are either; it is more likely that you are just human. So tell yourself the truth about you, too. It's only fair. You know you wouldn't want your kids beating themselves up that way. Don't you.

And lastly, figure out at least one thing you can do to make the current situation better. Do you need to make amends? Can you go back and repair the damage? How about a complete do-over? If the world did not already come to an end as a result of your mistake, then you probably have a chance to do something to fix it.

Once you get in the habit of doing this for yourself, it will be a lot easier to teach your children how to be gentle and honest with themselves, too.

NOTES

52. SUCCESS

And a Good Time Was Had by All

Success, sweet success! Who can resist its allure? We work for years to get our children to the point that they can taste it for themselves. And then, often as not, just like that they leave us. We remain behind, and they move on. We become their past, and they, the future we will never see. Sometimes, success for a parent is that moment when your child gets on the bus to head to college for the first time, and then just as you think your heart is about to break, at the very last moment he turns around on the steps. "Well, Mom, you did it," he quietly says. Then he turns, takes the last two steps into the dark interior, and is gone. Sometimes as quickly as that, this part of the parenting journey is over. They grow up. They leave home. They become adults.

For special-needs children, we may never have a leaving-home moment in quite that way. Their success may be moving to the independent living program. Voc-Rehab may help them find that first job. Or for some, that success they've worked so hard for may only be their beginning…

• •

Even though Shane had been told he had finally graduated, he continued, in his concrete thought, to insist that he did not have a real high school diploma, because, of course, he did not yet have the sheet of paper. It seemed it would never come. We had to provide them with the old special education diploma, which took a while because it had disappeared into the depths of the chaos in Shane's room. Then, once the school got the old one back, the replacement had to be ordered. After that, we had to wait months for the new one to come in.

For the entire time, Shane checked the mailbox religiously, every day, and he must have asked about it a dozen times more, each and every day. It was getting old. Those of us in his support group wanted to have a celebration at the school to give it to him, but he adamantly refused. He had already walked once, and he was NOT doing it again. Still, we thought anyone who had worked that hard deserved some kind of recognition.

Fortunately, when the diploma did finally come in, the school called me to come get it instead of mailing it. I immediately set wheels into motion. He had waited so long I could not in good conscience make him wait much longer, but something had to be done. The event was just too important to let it pass by unnoticed.

The diploma itself was whisked off to Tommy and Lauren's, so Lauren could frame it. Calls were made to doctors, family, friends: "A surprise party! Short notice! Can you come?"

Skip and Mimi graciously agreed to host the surprise, and enough people were able to come on short notice that all the major groups in Shane's life were at least represented. There was at least one person each from church, from the high school, from his medical support group, from family and friends.

We scheduled it on a Thursday, so Doc was able to come though Jeri could not. Mr. Dansby from the high school brought Mr. Kittrell and his seeing-eye dog. Shane's old tutor, Earline, came. Mauni, Martha, Nancy and her mother, Mae (who had provided after school care for Shane for his entire junior high and high school careers) were able to come from our old church. Brian, Beth and Patricia, and Dolly and Morgan were all able to attend. Friends Julie and Emily were there, and Bobby came by as soon as he got off of work. Jacob, Bridgett and I were the proud family members. But the stars of the show were Shane's tutor, Sherry Ware, and the new graduate and his diploma.

I dropped the unsuspecting graduate off at Doc's office for his regularly scheduled appointment, in order to give me time to get the party set up. We were almost organized when Tommy and Lauren got there, and Lauren realized she had forgotten the all-important diploma. While she raced back home to get it, I panicked about whether or not it would get there before Shane. Finally, Doc showed up with the graduate in tow, within minutes of her return.

We had "Congratulations Graduate" napkins and cake and punch, and it was a wonderful occasion. Sherry made a delightful presentation of the diploma to the graduate, and much to my astonishment Shane even made a little speech. It was a total surprise to all of us for him to say something in public, but he thanked everyone who came, and everyone who had helped him make it.

It was a night on which he was truly both Wonderful and Magnificent.

Skip and Mimi took pictures of Shane, the diploma, and each and every one of the people who attended the party. It was a short party, because Shane still doesn't like to stay up late. But it was glorious.

On the way home, he dropped the bombshell.

"Now, my second-next goal," he said with a grin, "is to graduate college. Not the four year one, just the two year one. I could do it one class at a time, on the Internet. I think I can make it."

And you know, he just might.

●●●

Consider...

What does success look like in your family of origin? How is it celebrated? How is it proclaimed? What parts of that ritual do you want to keep or throw away?

What would it take for you to feel you had successfully parented your child/ren? Would your young people have to meet your goals for them, or would it be enough for you if they met their own?

What if they can meet neither your goals for them *nor* their goals for themselves? Can you help them find something to celebrate in learning something new about themselves? Can you help reframe their lack of success in the conventional sense so that it becomes a successful experience nonetheless?

What can you do to help your child learn to celebrate the everyday successes as well as the big ones? Sometimes for someone who is depressed, for instance, just getting out of bed is a success. Can you help celebrate that, too?

Congratulations, You Did It.

Now, what are you going to do next?

NOTES

CONCLUSION

A Final Note on Foster Care, Adoption, and Court

*Court proceedings can be terrifying, empowering, or both, for children and for adults, too. If the child/ren you foster or adopt were abused in any way, they may well have had to testify in court before coming into your home. If court hearings take place while they are with you, your local victim advocacy service and your child's therapist can work together to prepare both you and your child/ren for the experience. The same people can also help everyone in your family process their intense feelings afterwards. If **you** go head-to-head with the state on your child's behalf, it may be you on the stand instead. That's not necessarily a bad thing. Some judges are inspirationally fair.*

About a half dozen of my favorite parenting moments have come during court hearings regarding Adoption Assistance contracts and the state. That's not to say it isn't anguish getting to that point; it is. And I know that winning isn't everything, but I do love it when my children receive the services they need. The best day of all though, hands down, was the day I wasn't even in court to fight for one of my own foster or adopted children.

It all came about as a result of a front-page article that the legislative reporter for our local paper had done on the failure of the state to honor its responsibility to provide the services one of my children had been promised. Brock desperately needed the services, but he wasn't getting them. I told the reporter about the situation, he reported it on the front page, and miraculously, the state decided to honor their contract and provide the needed services only days after the article appeared. Coincidence, I'm sure, but thank you one more time, Duren Cheek. I will always believe it was you and your articles that made it happen.

Anyway, an attorney at the local law school legal clinic had noticed the article, and some time later asked me to come testify as an expert witness in a case the legal clinic was representing. It turned out that the state and two foster parents had a conflict about what was in the best interest of the child those parents were fostering. The foster parents had asked the court to place the child in "permanent foster care" with them, their argument being that as long as the child *stayed* in foster care, the state *was* in fact providing for his needs. Their fear was that as soon as the child was adopted, that would cease to be the case. Since the child was profoundly multiply handicapped, they knew they were unable to assume financial responsibility for him. The bottom line was that they just did not trust the state. Permanent foster care would essentially make them the legal parents in every single respect other than financially. The state was fighting their request with every resource at its disposal. Its employees wanted to remove the child – who had been in the home for quite some time – because the foster parents refused to adopt the little boy.

So there I was, sitting in the back of the courtroom, waiting for my turn to testify, causing quite a stir. The state's attorney representing adoptions kept arguing that I should not be allowed to testify because this was not a case regarding one of my own children. The legal clinic attorney argued back that because of my personal experiences in this arena I was an expert witness. Back and forth they went, until finally the referee looked at me and asked, "What exactly is it that you have to tell me that they don't want me to hear?" It was just the opening I needed.

Without getting up from my seat, I told him the whole condensed version of my relationship with the state and the extremes I had been through to try to get the contracts enforced. I told him about having to declare bankruptcy because it took so long to get approvals for treatments the contracts guaranteed, and the foreclosure letters that followed. I talked about previous court battles, timely front-page articles that worked wonders, and about how all these struggles affected the children I had fostered and adopted. I went on for a pretty long time. When I was through, he pulled out a phone book.

I thought that was strange, since a court proceeding was going on, and was wondering what he was doing when he looked up at me again. "I can't find the number right now. Have you ever heard of Gordon Bonnyman and the Tennessee Justice Center?" he asked me.

"Sure," I grinned. Gordon had long before given me my own treasured copy of *The Runaway Bunny*. When he had done so, I was at the time exhausted and depleted from trying to hold on to children trying desperately hard to be rejected. The book was more of a comfort to me than he ever knew.

"Well, if they ever do this to you again," the referee went on, pointing at the state employees on the front row, "you should *sue* them."

It was gratifying. It was glorious. And it was a moment I will always remember.

••

Consider…

Would I ever want to do it again?

Don't you really think that loving even *one* child is enough to change the world?

How will *you* decide when you have reached *your* limit?

NOTES

Postscript

After the initial proof of this book was available, Shane's birth aunt, Wanda, read portions of it to his birth mother, Sandra. Sandra called me afterwards.

"Wanda read me parts of Shane's book," she began. "I cried when Wanda read it to me. Thank you for not giving up on him. I appreciate your being his mother and for you hanging in there with him. I'm glad Shane ended up with you," she told me. I was moved beyond words.

Not all foster or adoptive parents will ever receive a phone call like that. Many of us will never know our child's birth family, and many children will never realize just how much their parents sometimes long to hear a simple "thank you" for all they've done. While we may not love these children for the gratitude we might get someday, all of us deserve it. So…

On behalf of every mother who weeps in the dark,
unable to tend her own child,

THANK YOU.

On behalf of every father who cannot be there
when his child needs or wants to be loved,

THANK YOU.

On behalf of every social worker who has ever stayed up late worrying,
looking for just the right home for a child who needs one,

THANK YOU.

And on behalf of all those children desperately longing
for homes of their own,

THANK YOU MORE
THAN WORDS CAN SAY.

Photographs

Cover: Front: Shane (Photo by the author)
Back: The author (Photo by Ben Spiegel, Used by permission of Kathleen Nelson Spiegel)

Interior:

Page 2	Shane
Page 5	Tommy, Shane, and Ingrid
Page 8	Shane and Tasha at Shane's welcoming party (Photo by Allison and David Loebbaka)
Page 13	Shane
Page 15	Donnie, Shane, and Ronny (Photo by the author)
Page 20	Shane
Page 25	Tasha and Shane
Page 27	The author and Deborah (Photo by Douglas Bonar)
Page 30	Shane and Bobby
Page 33	The author and Shane (Photo by Allison and David Loebbaka)
Page 36	Shane
Page 39	Shane (Photo by the author)
Page 42	Shane and Tiko (Photo by Ingrid Bettis)
Page 45	Shane and the author (Photo taken at a YMCA dance)
Page 48	Shane (Photo by Allison and David Loebbaka)
Page 51	JR, Jessica, Shane, and Justin at Shane's birthday party
Page 54	Shane and Tasha
Page 57	Ingrid (Photo by the author)
Page 61	Shane and the author at Noel's high school graduation
Page 64	Brock
Page 65	Jacob (Photo by the author)
Page 68	Shane
Page 70	Christmas at Granny and Granddad's house: Back row: The author and Shane Front row: Brock and Jacob (Photo by Allison and David Loebbaka)
Page 71	Shane's little brothers: Brock, Jacob, and the twins, Donnie and Ronny (Photo by the author)
Page 73	Jonathan and Shane (Photo by Nancy Pigg)
Page 77	Top: Protesting Buddah/Shane (Photo by the author) Bottom: Shane in the back of the car singing "I've Got the Blues" (Photo by the author)
Page 80	Jacob and Brock's adoption day in court: Jacob, the author, Judge Robinson, Brock, and Shane (Photo by Skip and Mary Jo Boles)
Page 83	Shane and Rozita (Photo courtesy of Michael Horton Photographs)
Page 85	Shane and Patricia (Photo by Skip and Mary Jo Boles)
Page 88	Shane, Brock, Patricia, Jacob, and Brian (Photo by Skip and Mary Jo Boles)
Page 90	The author and Shane
Page 93	Shane, Earline, and Earline's grandson at Earline's college graduation (Photo by the author)
Page 98	Granny (Mae Webb) and Shane (Photo by Skip and Mary Jo Boles)
Page 101	Jacob, Brock, and Shane dressed for dinner on Valentine's Day (Photo taken at Sam's)
Page 104	Shane
Page 108	At the beach with Deb: Shane (standing) and Brock (buried in the sand) (Photo by the author)
Page 111	Shane, Brock, and Jacob (Photo by the author)
Page 114	Shane (Photo by the author)
Page 117	Clockwise from left: Lauren, Julie, Emily, Tommy, Shane, and Jacob (Photo by the author)
Page 118	Shane's "apartment" as it was found at Opryland
Page 122	Shane (Photo courtesy of Michael Horton Photographs)

Page 125 Shane's Kindergarten graduation
Page 128 Shane and his birth mother, Sandra Denise, at his high school graduation
Page 129 Sandra Denise with her rose (in her right hand) and Shane
Page 131 Jacob and Shane (Photo by Skip and Mary Jo Boles)
Page 134 Shane and Jonathan (Photo by the author)
Page 137 Sherry Ware (Photo by Skip and Mary Jo Boles)
Page 140 Shane (Photo by Skip and Mary Jo Boles)
Page 144 Top: Keo; Bottom: Shane's one and only soccer team, Shane standing far right
Page 146 Top: Mr. Dansby; Bottom: Mr. Kittrell and his seeing-eye dog (Photos by Skip and Mary Jo Boles)
Page 149 Shane (Photo by the author)
Page 152 Shane
Page 155 The author, Jacob, and Shane (Photo by "Grandma C." Revia Caruthers)
Page 158 Top: Sherry Ware, Shane, and the author
Center: Shane, the Diploma, and Nancy Pigg
Bottom: Shane, the diploma, and Jay (Photos by Skip and Mary Jo Boles)
Page 159 Top: Morgan, Shane, the diploma, and Jacob
Center: Brian, Patricia, Shane, the diploma, Beth, and Jo
Bottom: Shane, the diploma, and Sherry Ware (Photos by Skip and Mary Jo Boles)
Page 160 Top: Skip, Shane, the diploma, and Mimi
Bottom: Shane's "The Graduate" Card, noting the date we celebrated his actually receiving his regular high school diploma (Card courtesy of Doc)
Page 162 The author, her foster daughters, and her adopted sons: Standing: Brock, Shane, Mary, and Jacob; Sitting: Bridgett holding her son Zach, the author, and Rozita (Photo courtesy of Michael Horton Photographs)

THE AUTHOR WOULD LIKE TO THANK HER PARENTS
ALLISON AND DAVID LOEBBAKA

For Life, for Love, and for Scanning all the Photographs in this Book.

Also by Kate Rosemary

AFTER DISCLOSURE
A Non Offending Parent Reflects on Child Sexual Abuse

"A rare inside look at a non-offending parent's struggle with guilt, aloneness, shame and despair, and learning how to cope with these negative emotions. Demonstrating how to build a life for the victims that have been harmed so globally by the abuse, it is a story of the triumph over people's trauma and movement of a family into recovery."

Dr. Jay D. Woodman, Ph.D. Clinical and Consulting Psychology

"Five Stars. An absolutely powerful story, beautifully told. Having the ability to pick this up and connect with another parent who has walked in my shoes has been an amazing source of strength for me. This is an excellent book for other parents, students, and individuals within the system who are working to protect our children. A must read."

K. F., Non-Offending Parent of a Sexually Abused Child

"Required reading for all the perpetrators in our program. Furthermore, I think it ought to be required reading for everyone who works with cases of child sexual abuse in any profession."

John Brogden, Director, Association for Sexual Assault Prevention

"This book painfully and poetically describes the two years after the author discovered that the man she fell in love with and married was a pedophile. What happens to this family after the secret is out and they start to rebuild their dreams is not only maddening but a beautiful testament to courage, love and determination."

Bridgett Heil, R.N., Vanderbilt Children's Hospital

"Highly recommended: A unique story of personal, ecclesial and family narratives for all whose lives have been touched by pedophilia. This book forces the reader to take seriously the possibility of the pervasive nature of evil in a postmodern world. In the depth of its theological grounding, **After Disclosure** *is also appropriate for professionals who work with pedophiles – and for the abusers themselves."*

Rev. Peggy A. Way, Ph.D. Pastoral Care and Counseling

"This is not just a story for non-offending parents. This is a story for women who just can't 'like' their ex-husbands, for men who despise their bosses, and for people who hate the way southerners drive south of DC on I-95. This is an important story."

Elizabeth Wilson Jack

AN EXTRAORDINARY ACCOUNT of intergenerational abuse from the point of view of the non-offending parent, AFTER DISCLOSURE includes a study guide complete with questions appropriate for use by individuals, classes, and discussion groups.

To Order

RAISING SHANE

OR

AFTER DISCLOSURE
A NON OFFENDING PARENT REFLECTS ON CHILD SEXUAL ABUSE

Purchase Direct and Save 20%
Off the Original List Price of $24.95

Only $19.95 per copy after discount.

Include 9.25% tax for a total per copy price of $21.80
or provide proof of tax-exempt status.

Add $10/copy if you would like RAISING SHANE Spiral Bound.

Shipping and handling charge is $5.85 for the first book
***plus** $1 for each additional book.*

To Order by Mail, Send a Check or Money Order to:
Kate Rosemary
P.O. Box 605, Kingston Springs, Tennessee 37082

For faster service, credit or debit cards, use www.PayPal.com account:
kate.rosemary@recycleddreams.org

One free copy for the instructor or group leader is included
with every order of eleven or more books purchased
at the same time for the same mailing address.